INFOGRAPHIC

— GUIDE TO —

LITERATURE

Thunder Bay Press
An imprint of Printers Row Publishing Group
9717 Pacific Heights Blvd, San Diego, CA 92121
www.thunderbaybooks.com · mail@thunderbaybooks.com

Thunder Bay Press
Publisher: Peter Norton
Associate Publisher: Ana Parker
Editor: Dan Mansfield

Library of Congress Control Number: 2022941543

ISBN: 978-1-6672-0340-9

Printed in Singapore

26 25 24 23 22 1 2 3 4 5

INFOGRAPHIC

— GUIDE TO —

LITERATURE

FASCINATING FACTS AND FIGURES FOR BOOK LOVERS

Joanna Eliot

THUNDER BAY
P·R·E·S·S

San Diego, California

CONTENTS

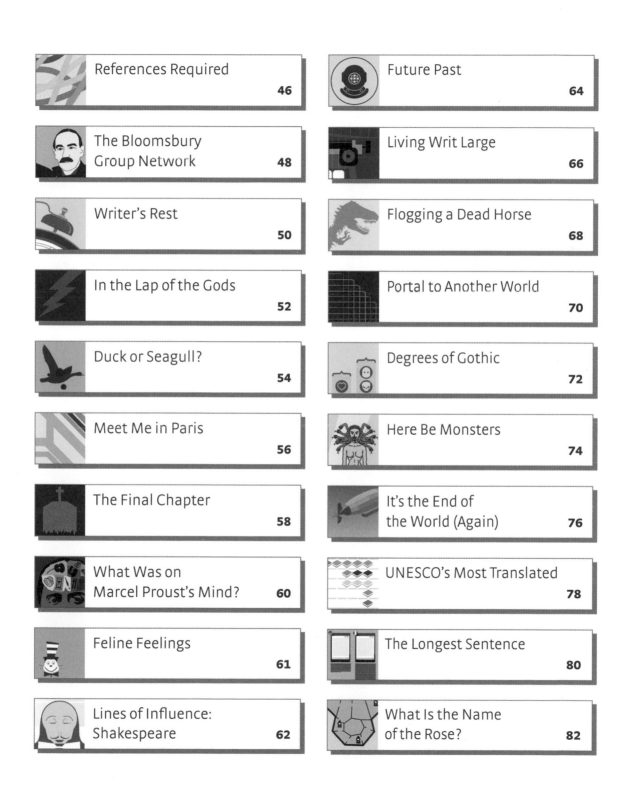

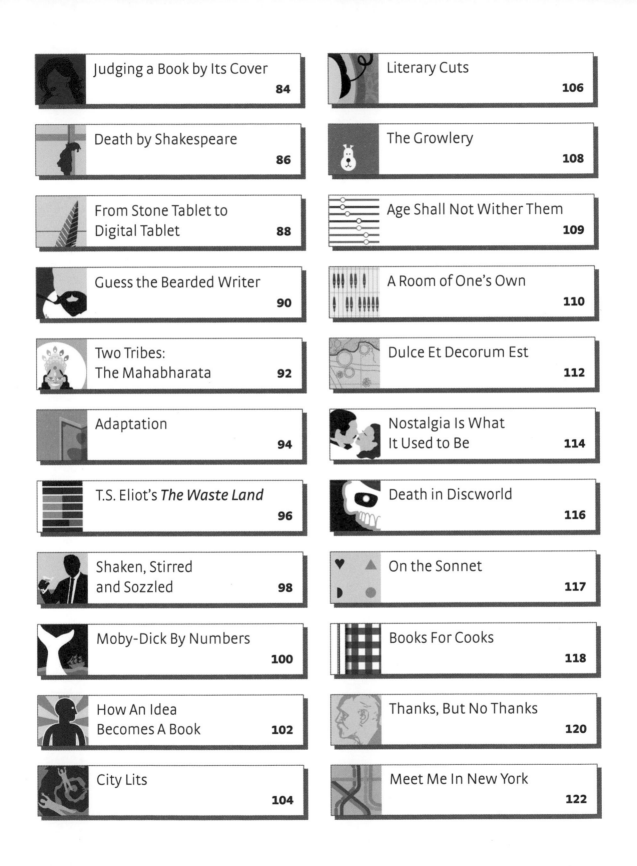

Introduction

BY JOANNA ELIOT

Being a self-confessed literature geek, my favourite non-fiction genre is the 'book about books'. So compiling this one in collaboration with other writers, and the very clever designer Gemma Wilson, was an exciting and endlessly fascinating undertaking. The possibilities for creating graphics was so potentially vast that we thought it safe to begin by answering simple questions such as: Who wrote the longest sentence ever published? What did famous writers do for a day job before they were famous? What were the common work routines of well-known writers? From there we moved on to answering more involved questions about gender-swapping authors, mother figures in literature of different cultures and the varying ways existential concepts are symbolized in fiction.

From the Greek myths to the worlds of *Cloud Atlas,* we have delved into the work of authors of all periods and genres, with spotlights on Shakespeare, Austen, Tolstoy, Umberto Eco, Pratchett's Discworld, *Moby-Dick*, crime writers of different nationalities, and many, many more. The works explored come from different continents and times, as well as drawing on publishing industry history and methods employed in creating cover design, rewrites and the politics of banned and stolen books.

Ever since its first publication in 1971, Gabriel García Márquez's masterpiece *One Hundred Years of Solitude* has been one of the most beloved works of fiction in the entire world. It won its author the Nobel Prize for Literature and no list of great novels is complete without it. To honour it, we depicted the sprawling family tree of strange and wonderful characters who people the town of Macondo.

However, because an infographic is so much more than just a visual representation of information, when created it can throw light onto often-unforeseen quirks of data. One of the things we discovered in making this book was that part of the beauty of the infographic is that it can suggest new meaning on texts that may not be so obvious in the original, written form.

Some of the information transformed into a graphic within these pages is reassuring, such as that most dogs in fiction are portrayed as faithful, heroic or loyal, rather than evil or ferocious, for instance. However, the infographic can also deliver something serendipitous and unexpected – such as in the comparative use of certain words in the works of Jane Austen and the Brontë sisters, or the most often reoccurring words in Tennyson's famous poem about death and mourning (*In Memoriam*) proving to be 'love', 'see', 'light' and 'life'.

Elsewhere we demonstrate the defining aspects of different cities via the literature set there, and in doing so show that Berlin-set novels are concerned with decadence and hedonism, Venice with disease, and Prague with identity crisis. Other graphics reveal patterns of similarity or difference between authors working in the same field of literature and at roughly the same time – so we find a loaded gun, often fired off stage, crops up in nearly every play by both Ibsen and Chekhov.

Finally, one of my very favourite pages to work on was the exploration in children's literature of the various portals into other worlds. There are many dramatic ways through, including the cyclone to Oz, a rabbit hole to Wonderland, or a trapdoor to Og, but the simplest and most understated way to another world was through the reading of a book, or being read aloud to. Which perhaps best sums up this book as a whole. I hope it serves to illustrate that reading literature is an infinite road of discovery and inspires you to explore the works of a new (or previously unread) author.

CRIMINAL **BODY COUNT**

When Agatha Christie introduced amateur detective spinster Jane Marple to the public in 1930, she began a trend in the crime genre for female authors to write about female detectives. Perhaps the most successful – and certainly longest-running – has been Patricia Cornwell's chief medical examiner, Kay Scarpetta. Comparing the body counts for the 12 Miss Marple novels against the first 12 (of 26) Kay Scarpetta gives an idea of how the world has changed since Murder At The Vicarage was published.

ISS MARPLE MISS MARPLE MISS MARPLE MISS MARPLE MISS MARPLE MISS MARPLE MIS

Murder At The Vicarage **1930** 1

The Body In The Library **1942** 2

The Moving Finger **1943** 2

A Murder Is Announced **1950** 4

They Do It With Mirrors **1952** 5

A Pocket Full Of Rye **1953** 3

4.50 From Paddington **1957** 3

The Mirror Crack'd **1962** 4

A Caribbean Mystery **1964** 3

At Bertram's Hotel **1965** 2

Nemesis **1971** 4

Sleeping Murder **1976** 2

AGATHA CHRISTIE
b.1890, Devon
d.1976, Oxfordshire,
England

TOTAL DEATHS 35

Postmortem **1990** 5

Body Of Evidence **1991** 4

All That Remains **1992** 13

Cruel And Unusual **1993** 8

The Body Farm **1994** 4

From Potter's Field **1995** 6

Cause Of Death **1996** 3

Unnatural Exposure **1997** 16

Point Of Origin **1998** 29

Black Notice **1999** 10

The Last Precinct **2000** 2

Blow Fly **2003** 5

PATRICIA CORNWELL
b.1956,
Miami, FL

KAY SCARPETTA KAY SCARPETTA KAY SCARPETTA KAY SCARPETTA KAY SCARPETTA KAY SCARP

number of deaths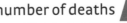

11

LITERARY **MISERY** INDEX

In 2013, researchers at University College London and Bristol University checked the occurrence of words that denoted misery in five million English-language works published between 1900 and 2000. They then checked their findings against the economically based US Misery Index, which charts unemployment and inflation. It seems that books get more miserable a decade after the world has undergone a depression.

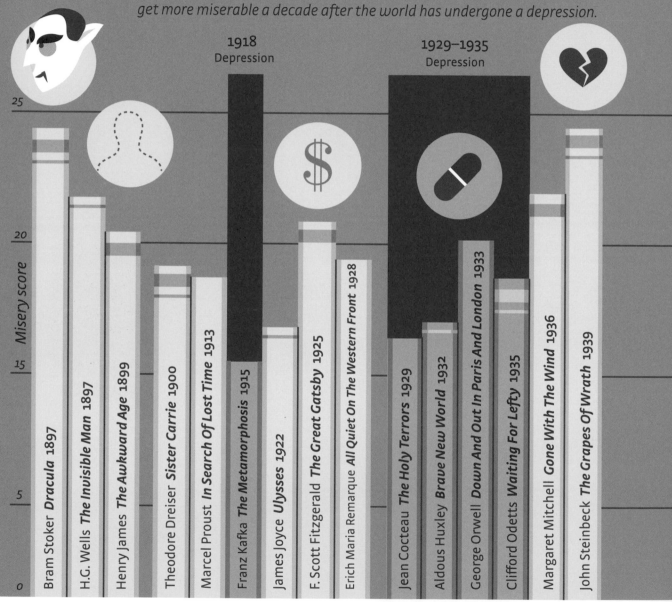

1918
Depression

1929–1935
Depression

Misery score

25

20

15

5

0

Bram Stoker *Dracula* 1897

H.G. Wells *The Invisible Man* 1897

Henry James *The Awkward Age* 1899

Theodore Dreiser *Sister Carrie* 1900

Marcel Proust *In Search Of Lost Time* 1913

Franz Kafka *The Metamorphosis* 1915

James Joyce *Ulysses* 1922

F. Scott Fitzgerald *The Great Gatsby* 1925

Erich Maria Remarque *All Quiet On The Western Front* 1928

Jean Cocteau *The Holy Terrors* 1929

Aldous Huxley *Brave New World* 1932

George Orwell *Down And Out In Paris And London* 1933

Clifford Odetts *Waiting For Lefty* 1935

Margaret Mitchell *Gone With The Wind* 1936

John Steinbeck *The Grapes Of Wrath* 1939

Late 19th century   **Early 20th century**   **During/Post-Great Depression**

1900

1950

Words searched for in groups noted as:

| anger | disgust | fear | joy | surprise |

1975–1980
Depression

Primo Levi *If This Is A Man* 1947

Allen Ginsberg *Howl* 1955

Ayn Rand *Atlas Shrugged* 1957

William S. Burroughs *The Naked Lunch* 1959

Ken Kesey *One Flew Over The Cuckoo's Nest* 1962

Sylvia Plath *The Bell Jar* 1963

Martin Amis *Money* 1984

Milan Kundera *The Unbearable Lightness Of Being* 1984

Toni Morrison *Beloved* 1987

Tom Wolfe *The Bonfire Of The Vanities* 1987

Bret Easton Ellis *American Psycho* 1991

Douglas Coupland *Generation X* 1991

Michel Houellebecq *Platform* 2001

Karl Ove Knausgaard *A Time To Every Purpose Under Heaven* 2004

Cormac McCarthy *The Road* 2006

Post-war   *1980s*   *21st century*

Bentley RA, Acerbi A, Ormerod P, Lampos V (2014) Books Average Previous Decade of Economic Misery.
PLoS ONE 9(1): e83147. doi:10.1371/journal.pone.0083147

HEINE'S GERMANY:
A WINTER'S TALE

The work of German-Jewish poet Heinrich Heine was banned in his homeland in 1835. In 1844, inspired by composer Schubert's Die Winterreise, *Heine published* Deutschland: Ein Wintermärchen, *an imaginary journey through his homeland in poetic form. Here's where he went and the symbolic items of each section.*

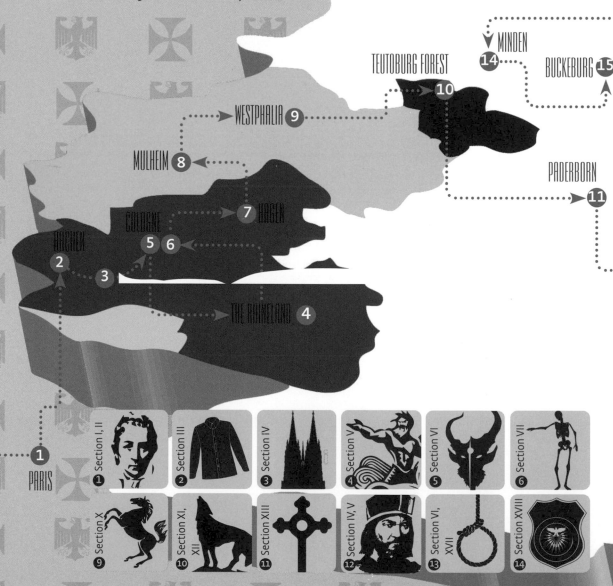

MINDEN 14

BUCKEBURG 15

TEUTOBURG FOREST 10

WESTPHALIA 9

PADERBORN 11

MULHEIM 8

COLOGNE 5 6 — 7 HAGEN

AACHEN 2

3

THE RHINELAND 4

1 PARIS

Section I, II ①
Section III ②
Section IV ③
Section V ④
Section VI ⑤
Section VII ⑥
Section X ⑨
Section XI, XII ⑩
Section XIII ⑪
Section IV, V ⑫
Section VI, XVII ⑬
Section XVIII ⑭

16 HAMBURG

13

12

KYFFHÄUSER

Section VIII

Section IX

Section XIX

Section XX–XXVII

KEY TO SYMBOLS

1 START: (Section I, II) Paris; Heine sets out on an imaginary journey to real places.

2 (Section III) Aachen; lands in Germany carrying shirts, trousers, handkerchiefs in a suitcase and books in his head.

3 (Section IV) Travels the road from Aachen to Cologne, and at Cologne Cathedral applauds the unfinished building as showing Germany's progressive society.

4 (Section V) In the Rhineland, Heine sees old Father Rhine as sad and disappointed with Germans concerned about their identity.

5 (Section VI) Cologne; Heine shows 'Liktor' a demon who is always with him and carries a hatchet under his cloak.

6 (Section VII) At Cologne Cathedral Heine smashes the 'skeletons of superstition'.

7 (Section VIII) Hagen; Heine recalls seeing Napoleon Bonaparte's funeral.

8 (Section IX) Mulheim; Heine recalls the taste of great sauerkraut.

9 (Section X) Heine sends his regards to Westphalia.

10 (Section XI, XII) Heine travels through Teutoburg Forest, imagining Germany if the Romans had remained; at night he hears the wolves howl.

11 (Section XIII) Paderborn; a crucifix appears in the mist.

12 (Section IV, V) In a dream at Kyffhäuser, Heine sees Barbarossa, Roman Emperor and King of Germany, as a senile old man.

13 (Section XVI, XVII) Still at Kyffhäuser, Heine considers the guillotine, noose and sword as redundant for emperors now that the people rule.

14 (Section XVIII) At Minden, Heine is detained by the police.

15 (Section XIX) Heine visits his grandfather's birthplace at Bückeburg and meets Augustus I of Hanover.

16 (Section XX—XXVII) Heine finally arrives in Hamburg where he sees his mother, before walking around the city and meditating on how things can be and how they will end.

wikipedia.org

ONE HUNDRED YEARS OF SOLITUDE
FAMILY TREE

Colombian Gabriel García Márquez's novel was first published in Spanish in 1967, and has since been translated into more than 46 languages and sold over 47 million copies. This family tree offers a guide to the complex tale of six generations who are destined to repeat history.

Rebeca
Adopted orphan, marries José, eats earth

José Arcadio
First-born, enormous, covered in tattoos

Pilar Ternera

Santa Sofía de la Piedad
Wife of Arcadio, the transient, maternal member of the family

Arcadio
Proves a vicious dictator of Macondo during the uprising

Remedios the Beauty
Most beautiful woman in the world. Abruptly leaves the novel after floating to heaven

José Arcadio Segundo
Becomes a reclusive scholar; sole survivor of the massacre of the strikers against the banana company

Petra Cotes

Gaston
Husband of Amaranta Úrsula, travels to Belgium and never returns

Amaranta Úrsula
Dies in childbirth when delivering the incestuous child of her nephew Aureliano (II)

José Arcadio Buendía
Patriarch, founder of Macondo

Úrsula Iguarán
Wife to José, lives to be 130

Colonel Aurellano Buendía
Second son, warrior, artist, father to 17 sons

RIP

Remedios Moscote
Wife to Colonel Buendía, dies during first pregnancy

Amaranta
Third child, dies a lonely spinster

Aureliano José
Obsessed with his aunt Amaranta

17 Aurelianos

Aureliano Segundo
Immense, boisterous and impulsive

Fernanda del Carpio
Strong religious views which she imposes

José Arcadio II - groomed to become Pope, slips into a life of debauchery after an unsuccessful trip to seminary

Meme - real name Renata Remedios, proves hedonistic like her father, lives out her life imprisoned in a convent after her affair with Mauricio

Aureliano II
Grows from a hermit to a scholar, and deciphers the prophecies of Melquíades. Fathers the last of the Buendía line with his aunt

Aureliano III
Incestuous child of Aureliano II and Amaranta Úrsula, who is born with the tail of a pig

AUSTEN VS. **BRONTË**

Were Jane Austen and the Brontë sisters obsessed with bonnets, balls, dresses, marriage and matters of the heart? A search for key words in the collected novels of each show intriguing differences between works by the same authors.

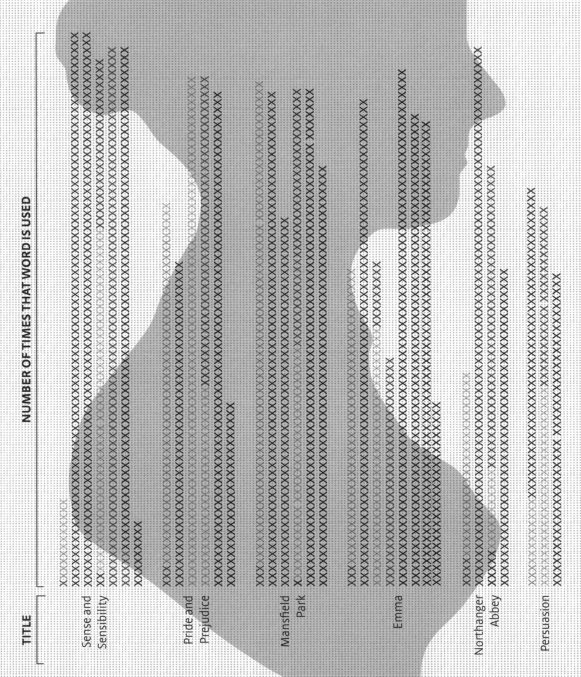

NUMBER OF TIMES THAT WORD IS USED

TITLE

Sense and Sensibility
Pride and Prejudice
Mansfield Park
Emma
Northanger Abbey
Persuasion

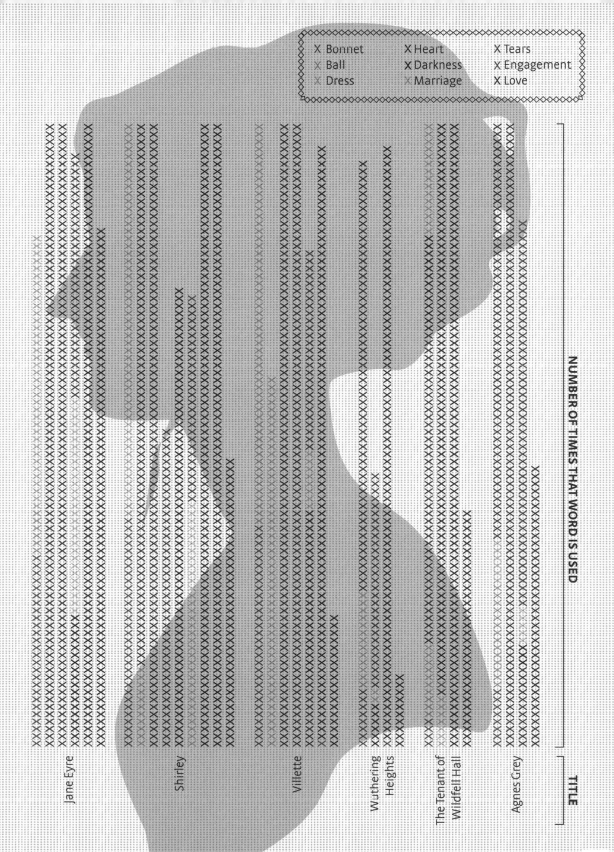

Legend:
- X Bonnet
- X Ball
- X Dress
- X Heart
- X Darkness
- X Marriage
- X Tears
- X Engagement
- X Love

NUMBER OF TIMES THAT WORD IS USED

Titles:
- Jane Eyre
- Shirley
- Villette
- Wuthering Heights
- The Tenant of Wildfell Hall
- Agnes Grey

STEAL THIS BOOK

Books get stolen from libraries – where you can take them away for free – and bookshops in their thousands every year. What gets stolen varies from city to city, place to place, but the libraries all seem to suffer from thieves with the same desires.

NEW YORK BOOKSHOPS

TITLE	AUTHOR
All	Charles Bukowski
All	William Burroughs
On The Road	Jack Kerouac
The New York Trilogy	Paul Auster
All	Martin Amis
All	Jim Thompson
All	Philip K. Dick
All	Michel Foucault
All	Hunter S. Thompson
Graphic novels	Various

WORLD LIBRARIES

TITLE	AUTHOR	PLACE
The Bible	Various	
Wicca and witchcraft titles	Various	
Guinness World Records	Various	
Harry Potter (all)	J.K. Rowling	
Fifty Shades Of Grey (all)	E.L. James	
Exam prep guides	Various	
Art reference books	Various	
The Kama Sutra	Vatsyayana	
Business advice manuals	Various	
Swimsuit Annual	Sports Illustrated	

INTERNATIONAL SHOPLIFTING COSTS

COUNTRY	COST
USA	$41.7 billion
Japan	$9.6 billion
UK	$7.8 billion
Germany	$7.3 billion
France	$6.3 billion
Italy	$4.7 billion
Russia	$4 billion
Spain	$3.9 billion
Canada	$3.6 billion
Australia	$2 billion

LONDON BOOKSHOPS

TITLE	AUTHOR
London A–Z	Geographer's A–Z Map Co.
Lonely Planet Europe	Various
The Guv'nor	Lenny McLean
Tintin (all)	Hergé
Asterix (all)	Goscinny & Uderzo
Steal This Book	Abbie Hoffman
Spider-Man	Stan Lee
Wall And Piece	Banksy
Moleskin diaries (stationery)	n/a
The Virgin Suicides	Jeffrey Eugenides

SCOTLAND BOOKSHOPS

TITLE	AUTHOR	PLACE
Harry Potter And The Chamber Of Secrets	J.K. Rowling	
Lovers And Players	Jackie Collins	
Diamond Girls	Jacqueline Wilson	
Rebus (all)	Ian Rankin	
DSA Driving Theory	HMSO	
Street Child	Berlie Doherty	
Charlie And The Chocolate Factory	Roald Dahl	
Discworld (all)	Terry Pratchett	
All	Stephen King	
All	Agatha Christie	

guardian.com, dailyrecord.com, huffingtonpost.com, publishersweekly.org, wikipedia

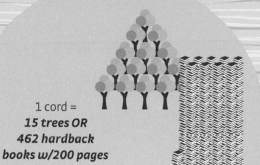

WOOD FOR **BOOKS**

Publishing isn't the greenest of industries, what with the vast majority of its key product being made of paper. Exactly how many trees each year get turned into books?

1 cord =
**15 trees OR
462 hardback
books w/200 pages**

1 cord of air-dried dense hardwood =
300 reams of paper

1 tree = **31 books**

At 31 books per tree that = **645 million trees in total each year to make books**

UNESCO calculates 2 million titles published annually with a varying print run =
2 billion books printed

Percentage of **paper generated from recycling** worldwide

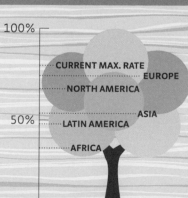

- 100%
- CURRENT MAX. RATE
- EUROPE
- NORTH AMERICA
- ASIA
- LATIN AMERICA
- 50%
- AFRICA
- 0%

Number of times **paper fibres are recycled** worldwide

7 times
Max. possible with current technlogy

3.8 times
Europe

2.4 times
World average

ecology.com, unesco.org, ehow.com, dataworldbank.org

THE MOST EXPENSIVE
RARE BOOKS

Rare books that
command a price in
the millions of dollars
tend to be one-off
productions, often
handwritten and
very old.

2007
The First Book Of Urizen
1794 William Blake

The Timurid Quran
c15th

The Bomberg Babylonian Talmud
c16th

The Canterbury Tales
Geoffrey Chaucer
1476–1478

Philosophiae Naturalis Principia Mathematica
Isaac Newton
1686

Don Quixote
Miguel De Cervantes
1605–1615

St Cuthbert Gospel
Unknown
c7th

Geographia Cosmographia
Claudius Ptolemy
1478

Birds Of America
John James Audubon
1827–1838

The Gutenberg Bible
Various
1456

The Bay Psalm Book
Various
1640

Handwritten

The Bo
Joseph S

Alice's Adventures
In Wonderland
1830   **1865** Lewis Carroll

The Rothschild Prayerbook
Unknown
1500–1520

First Folio
William Shakespeare
1623

The Gospels Of Henry The Lion
Order of St Benedict monks
c12th

De Revolutionibus Orbium Coelestium
Nicolaus Copernicus
1543

Magna Carta
Unknown
1297

The Codex Leicester
Leonardo da Vinci
C15th

| 600 | ... | 1100 | 1250 | 1300 | 1350 | 1400 | 1450 | 1500 | 1550 | 1600 | 1650 | 1700 | 1750 | 1800 | 1850 | 1900 | 1950 | 2000 | 2050 |

PUBLISHED/WRITTEN

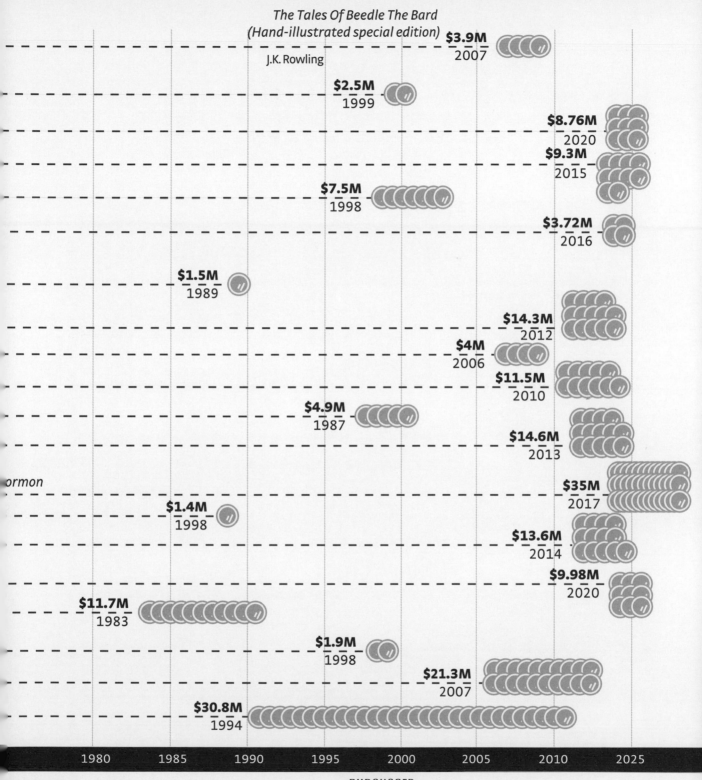

The Tales Of Beedle The Bard
(Hand-illustrated special edition)

J.K. Rowling

$3.9M
2007

$2.5M
1999

$8.76M
2020

$9.3M
2015

$7.5M
1998

$3.72M
2016

$1.5M
1989

$14.3M
2012

$4M
2006

$11.5M
2010

$4.9M
1987

$14.6M
2013

ormon

$35M
2017

$1.4M
1998

$13.6M
2014

$9.98M
2020

$11.7M
1983

$1.9M
1998

$21.3M
2007

$30.8M
1994

| 1980 | 1985 | 1990 | 1995 | 2000 | 2005 | 2010 | 2025 |

PURCHASED

wikicollecting.org, 1stedition.net, abebooks.com, wikipedia.org

YOU **MUST** HAVE READ THIS...

The best-selling books in the world – excepting religious tomes – include some of the best-known novels of all time. Here are the books, some published many centuries ago, that have sold from tens to hundreds of millions of copies.

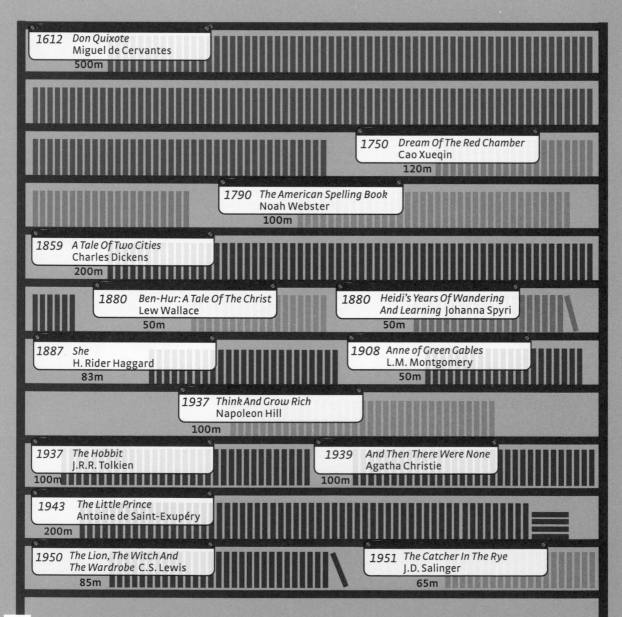

1612 *Don Quixote*
Miguel de Cervantes
500m

1750 *Dream Of The Red Chamber*
Cao Xueqin
120m

1790 *The American Spelling Book*
Noah Webster
100m

1859 *A Tale Of Two Cities*
Charles Dickens
200m

1880 *Ben-Hur: A Tale Of The Christ*
Lew Wallace
50m

1880 *Heidi's Years Of Wandering And Learning* Johanna Spyri
50m

1887 *She*
H. Rider Haggard
83m

1908 *Anne of Green Gables*
L.M. Montgomery
50m

1937 *Think And Grow Rich*
Napoleon Hill
100m

1937 *The Hobbit*
J.R.R. Tolkien
100m

1939 *And Then There Were None*
Agatha Christie
100m

1943 *The Little Prince*
Antoine de Saint-Exupéry
200m

1950 *The Lion, The Witch And The Wardrobe* C.S. Lewis
85m

1951 *The Catcher In The Rye*
J.D. Salinger
65m

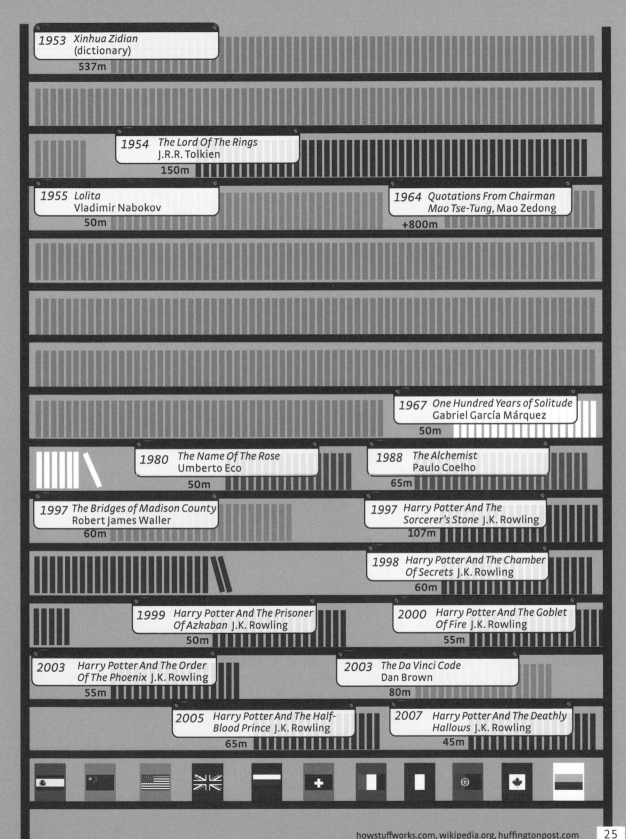

1953 *Xinhua Zidian* (dictionary)
537m

1954 *The Lord Of The Rings* J.R.R. Tolkien
150m

1955 *Lolita* Vladimir Nabokov
50m

1964 *Quotations From Chairman Mao Tse-Tung*, Mao Zedong
+800m

1967 *One Hundred Years of Solitude* Gabriel García Márquez
50m

1980 *The Name Of The Rose* Umberto Eco
50m

1988 *The Alchemist* Paulo Coelho
65m

1997 *The Bridges of Madison County* Robert James Waller
60m

1997 *Harry Potter And The Sorcerer's Stone* J.K. Rowling
107m

1998 *Harry Potter And The Chamber Of Secrets* J.K. Rowling
60m

1999 *Harry Potter And The Prisoner Of Azkaban* J.K. Rowling
50m

2000 *Harry Potter And The Goblet Of Fire* J.K. Rowling
55m

2003 *Harry Potter And The Order Of The Phoenix* J.K. Rowling
55m

2003 *The Da Vinci Code* Dan Brown
80m

2005 *Harry Potter And The Half-Blood Prince* J.K. Rowling
65m

2007 *Harry Potter And The Deathly Hallows* J.K. Rowling
45m

THE ORIGINAL DHARMA **DRAMA**

The Indian epic poem The Ramayana *was written in 1000 BCE and remains one of the most read, interpreted and staged poems in the world. The story shares key aspects of plot with those of Homer, with families warring, wives abducted and gods in human form.*

JATAYU
Allied to Rama, a demi-god in the form of a vulture. Attempts to foil Ravana's kidnapping of Sita, gets his wings chopped off. Lives long enough to inform Rama.

SITA
Wife of Rama, incarnation of the Goddess of Wealth, Laxmi. Absolutely devoted to her husband, supremely chaste, willing to undergo test of fire to prove her purity. When driven into exile she is absorbed by Mother Earth.

HANUMAN
Allied to Rama, son of the God of Wind, Vayu, half-monkey half-man he has super strength and the ability to fly, and to grow to any size he wants. Carried a mountain on his back and set a city on fire using his tail as a torch.

DASHARATHA
Father and King of Ayodhya, undertook a ritual by the God of Fire so that his three wives would bear great progeny.

LAKSHMANA
Youngest son, loyal to Rama. Good with a bow and sword, great sidekick.

SRAMA
First-born son, incarnation of the god Vishnu. Embodies duty and honour (dharma). Destroyer of demons, possesses divine weaponry and super-strength. Reigned for 11,000 golden years, without war, calamity or disease. Weakness: the poison of a particular snake was said to put him into a coma.

VIBHISHANA
The demon brother of Ravana with a heart of gold. He urged Ravana to return Sita to her husband, and when Ravana refused, he sided with Rama's army and helped their victory. Was crowned the King of Lanka after Ravana's defeat and is a symbol of inherent good triumphing against all odds.

THE GOOD GUYS

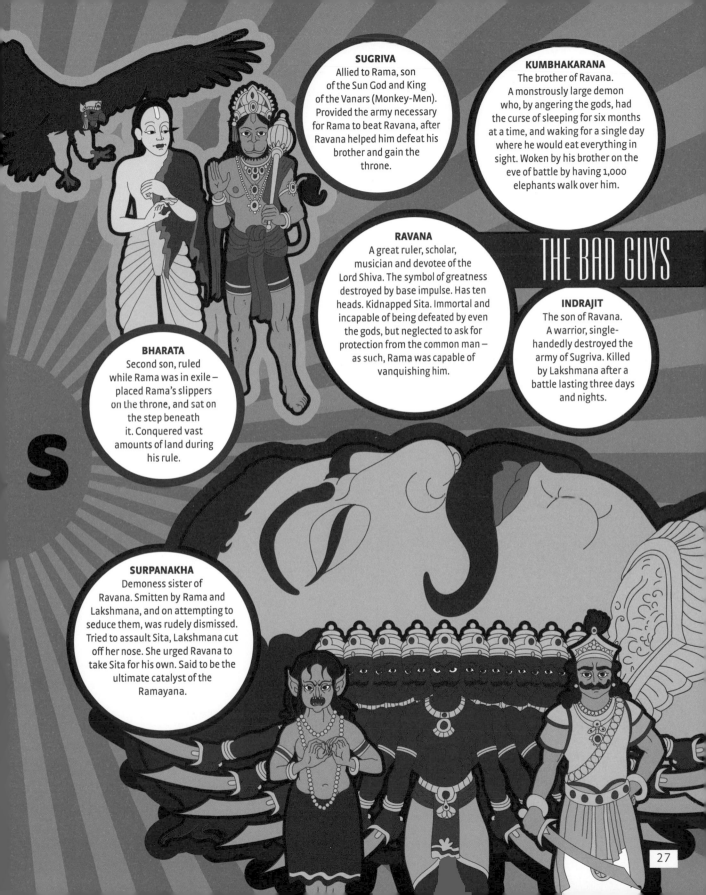

SUGRIVA
Allied to Rama, son of the Sun God and King of the Vanars (Monkey-Men). Provided the army necessary for Rama to beat Ravana, after Ravana helped him defeat his brother and gain the throne.

KUMBHAKARANA
The brother of Ravana. A monstrously large demon who, by angering the gods, had the curse of sleeping for six months at a time, and waking for a single day where he would eat everything in sight. Woken by his brother on the eve of battle by having 1,000 elephants walk over him.

RAVANA
A great ruler, scholar, musician and devotee of the Lord Shiva. The symbol of greatness destroyed by base impulse. Has ten heads. Kidnapped Sita. Immortal and incapable of being defeated by even the gods, but neglected to ask for protection from the common man — as such, Rama was capable of vanquishing him.

THE BAD GUYS

INDRAJIT
The son of Ravana. A warrior, single-handedly destroyed the army of Sugriva. Killed by Lakshmana after a battle lasting three days and nights.

BHARATA
Second son, ruled while Rama was in exile – placed Rama's slippers on the throne, and sat on the step beneath it. Conquered vast amounts of land during his rule.

SURPANAKHA
Demoness sister of Ravana. Smitten by Rama and Lakshmana, and on attempting to seduce them, was rudely dismissed. Tried to assault Sita, Lakshmana cut off her nose. She urged Ravana to take Sita for his own. Said to be the ultimate catalyst of the Ramayana.

TAKE FOUR **DETECTIVES...**

Written by novelists from four different countries, all of whom have been best-sellers and made into television stars, mix and see what emerges.

DETECTIVE PEPE CARVALHO

Setting: Barcelona, Spain

Profile: Middle-aged, unorthodox private investigator, former Communist and CIA agent, burns books for warmth, has a difficult relationship with girlfriend, cooks complicated meals.

Country of author: Spain	
Creator: Manuel Vázquez Montalbán	
Novels: 18	1972–2004
Short story collections: 4	1987
Recipe books: 1	1989
Sales: 2m in Spanish language	

Carvalho TV series:
(Spain) 3, 18 episodes, 1986–2003

Carvalho movies:
(Spain) 2, 1995, 1997;
(Italy) 4, 1976, 1983, 1990, 1991

INSPECTOR KURT WALLANDER

Setting: Ystad, Sweden

Profile: Middle-aged, unorthodox senior police officer, divorced, ailing father, has a complicated relationship with girlfriend, lives on the beach, cooks simple meals, falls asleep in an armchair.

Country of author: Sweden	
Creator: Henning Mankell	
Novels: 11	1997–2011
Sales: 30m in 40 languages	

Wallander TV series:
(Sweden) 3, 32 episodes, 2005–2013;
(UK) 4, 12 episodes 2008–2015

Young Wallander (Sweden/UK), 2, 12 episodes 2020–

Wallander movies:
(Sweden) 9, 1994–2007

COMMISSARIO SALVO MONTALBANO

Setting: Sicily, Italy

Profile: Middle-aged, unorthodox senior police officer, has a complicated relationship with girlfriend, lives on the beach, swims, cooks complicated meals.

Country of author: Italy	
Creator: Andrea Camilleri	
Novels: 28	1994–2019
Short story collections: 9	1998–2018
Sales: 16.5m in 30 languages	
Montalbano TV series: (Italy) 15, 37 episodes, 1999–2021	
Prequel TV episodes: (Italy) 2, 12 episodes, 2012–2015	

DETECTIVE AURELIO ZEN

Setting: Perugia, Rome and Sardinia, Italy

Profile: Middle-aged, unorthodox senior police officer, has a complicated relationship with girlfriend, an ailing mother, likes to cook simple pasta dishes.

Country of author: England	
Creator: Michael Dibden	
Novels: 11	1998–2007
Sales: 1m+ copies in 18 languages	
Zen TV series: (UK) 1, 3 episodes, 2011	

GIVING UP THE **DAY JOB**

Writers become professional when they have sold enough books to be able to guarantee that the bills will be paid, so they write in their spare time, while working at a 'day job'. Here's what several successful authors would have been earning if they'd continued with their first occupation, and what they or their estate is worth now.

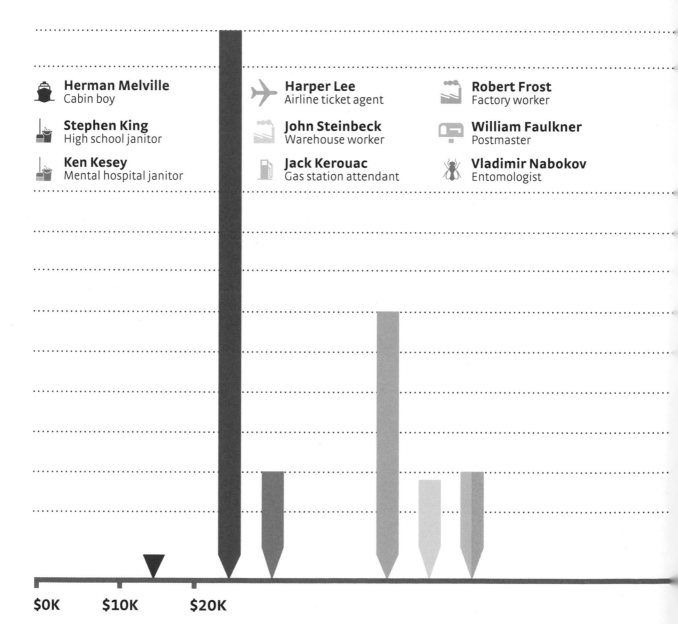

Herman Melville
Cabin boy

Stephen King
High school janitor

Ken Kesey
Mental hospital janitor

Harper Lee
Airline ticket agent

John Steinbeck
Warehouse worker

Jack Kerouac
Gas station attendant

Robert Frost
Factory worker

William Faulkner
Postmaster

Vladimir Nabokov
Entomologist

$0K $10K $20K

SALARY AT ORIGINAL JOB

$1Bn

$400M

$200M

William S. Burroughs
Pest control technician

J.K. Rowling
Researcher (Amnesty Intl)

Kurt Vonnegut
Manager, US Saab dealership

Stieg Larsson
Graphic designer

J.D. Salinger
Entertainment director

John Grisham
Lawyer

$50M

$45M

$40M

$35M

$25M

$20M

$15M

$10M

$5M

SALARY AS AN AUTHOR

$30K $40K $50K $60K $70K

SALARY AT ORIGINAL JOB

MOTHER DEAREST?

Family matters are a major theme in the great novels of the 19th and early 20th centuries. From Jane Austen to Virginia Woolf, via Charles Dickens, George Eliot, Oscar Wilde, D.H. Lawrence and E.M. Forster, the role of the mother was minutely examined and often found wanting. Here's how the mothers in the major works of each author measure up, as either good, bad, or simply dead.

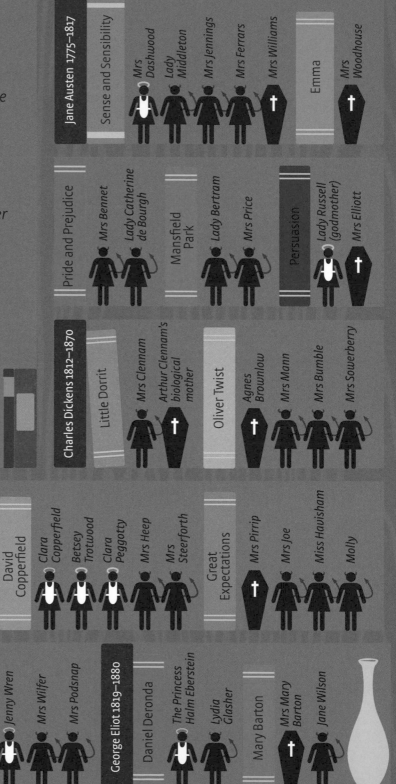

Jane Austen 1775–1817

Sense and Sensibility — Mrs Dashwood, Lady Middleton, Mrs Jennings, Mrs Ferrars, Mrs Williams

Emma — Mrs Woodhouse

Pride and Prejudice — Mrs Bennet, Lady Catherine de Bourgh

Mansfield Park — Lady Bertram, Mrs Price

Persuasion — Lady Russell (godmother), Mrs Elliott

Charles Dickens 1812–1870

Little Dorrit — Mrs Clennam, Arthur Clennam's biological mother

Oliver Twist — Agnes Brownlow, Mrs Mann, Mrs Bumble, Mrs Sowerberry

The Old Curiosity Shop — Mrs Trent

Nicholas Nickleby — Mrs Nickleby, Mrs Squeers, Mrs Witterly

David Copperfield — Clara Copperfield, Betsey Trotwood, Clara Pegotty, Mrs Heep, Mrs Steerforth

Great Expectations — Mrs Pirrip, Mrs Joe, Miss Havisham, Molly

Bleak House — Honoria, Lady Dedlock, Mrs Barbary, Mrs Jellyby

Our Mutual Friend — Mrs Henrietta Boffin, Jenny Wren, Mrs Wilfer, Mrs Podsnap

George Eliot 1819–1880

Daniel Deronda — The Princess Halm Eberstein, Lydia Glasher

Mary Barton — Mrs Mary Barton, Jane Wilson

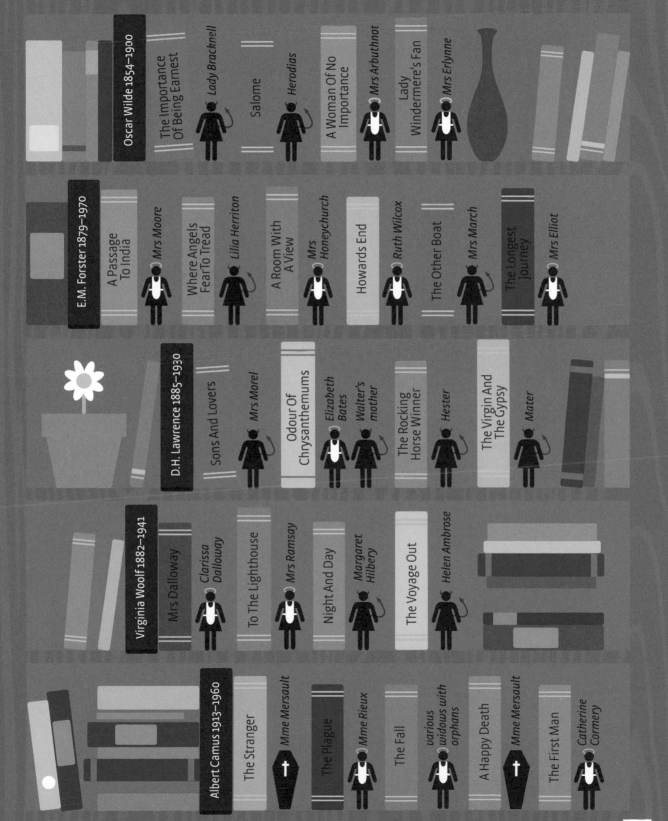

Oscar Wilde 1854–1900

The Importance Of Being Earnest — *Lady Bracknell*

Salome — *Herodias*

A Woman Of No Importance — *Mrs Arbuthnot*

Lady Windermere's Fan — *Mrs Erlynne*

E.M. Forster 1879–1970

A Passage To India — *Mrs Moore*

Where Angels Fear To Tread — *Lilia Herriton*

A Room With A View — *Mrs Honeychurch*

Howards End — *Ruth Wilcox*

The Other Boat — *Mrs March*

The Longest Journey — *Mrs Elliot*

D.H. Lawrence 1885–1930

Sons And Lovers — *Mrs Morel*

Odour Of Chrysanthemums — *Elizabeth Bates*, *Walter's mother*

The Rocking Horse Winner — *Hester*

The Virgin And The Gypsy — *Mater*

Virginia Woolf 1882–1941

Mrs Dalloway — *Clarissa Dalloway*

To The Lighthouse — *Mrs Ramsay*

Night And Day — *Margaret Hilbery*

The Voyage Out — *Helen Ambrose*

Albert Camus 1913–1960

The Stranger — *Mme Mersault*

The Plague — *Mme Rieux*

The Fall — *various widows with orphans*

A Happy Death — *Mme Mersault*

The First Man — *Catherine Cormery*

33

BANNED
BOOKS

REASON WHY

HOMOSEXUAL CONTENT
HELIOCENTRIC HERESY
SEXUAL OBSCENITY
HERETICAL

PRO-DEMOCRATIC

OBSCENITY

DEPRAVED, IMMORAL, PSYCHOTIC, VULGAR, ANTI-CHRISTIAN
RACIALLY OFFENSIVE
LIBELLOUS, PRO- COMMUNIST
PRO- COMMUNIST
SEX, OBSCENITY
PROFANITY
OFFENSIVE LANGUAGE

VIOLENCE
ENCOURAGING PROMISCUITY

ANTI-COMMUNIST
GLORIFYING ROYAL FAMILIES
INCLUSION OF TALKING PIGS
CRITICISM OF GOVERNMENT
ANTHROPOMORPHIC ANIMALS

ANTI-ISLAMIC/ OFFENSIVE TO ISLAM

OFFENSIVE TO ISLAM

TITLE AND WRITER

Poetry On Love And Longing, Sappho
Dialogue Concerning The Two Chief World Systems, Galileo Galilei
The Hunchback of Notre-Dame, Victor Hugo
The Bible, Various/Martin Luther
Paradise Lost, John Milton
Tyndale Bible, Various/John Tyndale
Maya Codices, Various
The Talmud, Various
The Odyssey, Homer

Lolita, Vladimir Nabokov

Ars Amatoria, Ovid

Ulysses, James Joyce
Lady Chatterley's Lover, D.H. Lawrence

The Color Purple, Alice Walker

Howl, Allen Ginsberg
Huckleberry Finn, Mark Twain

Slaughterhouse-Five, Kurt Vonnegut

The Grapes Of Wrath, John Steinbeck
American Psycho, Bret Easton Ellis
The Catcher In The Rye, J.D. Salinger
I Know Why The Caged Bird Sings, Maya Angelou
Bridge To Terabithia, Katherine Paterson
Catch-22, Joseph Heller
The Adventures Of Captain Underpants, Dav Pilkey
Brave New World, Aldous Huxley

Animal Farm, George Orwell

Fairy Tales, Hans Christian Andersen
Alice's Adventures In Wonderland, Lewis Carroll

The Satanic Verses, Salman Rushdie

Harry Potter series, J.K. Rowling

21st centuries, here are the 30 most infamous
– and sometimes surprising – books to have
been banned from public consumption.

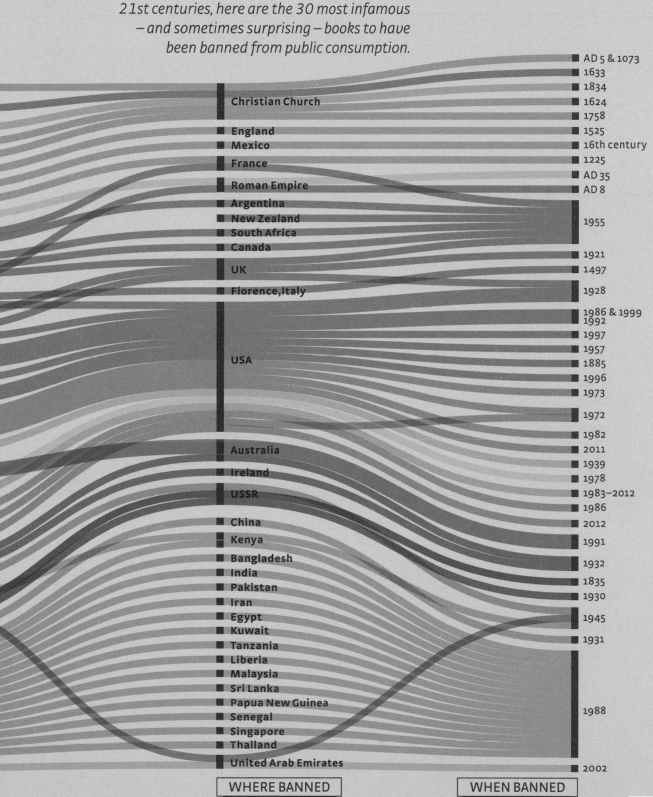

WHERE BANNED	WHEN BANNED

Christian Church — AD 5 & 1073, 1633, 1834, 1624, 1758
England — 1525
Mexico — 16th century
France — 1225
Roman Empire — AD 35, AD 8
Argentina
New Zealand — 1955
South Africa
Canada
UK — 1921, 1497
Florence, Italy — 1928
USA — 1986 & 1999, 1992, 1997, 1957, 1885, 1996, 1973, 1972, 1982
Australia — 2011, 1939
Ireland — 1978
USSR — 1983–2012, 1986
China — 2012
Kenya — 1991
Bangladesh — 1932
India — 1835, 1930
Pakistan
Iran
Egypt — 1945
Kuwait — 1931
Tanzania
Liberia
Malaysia
Sri Lanka
Papua New Guinea
Senegal — 1988
Singapore
Thailand
United Arab Emirates — 2002

ala.org, oif.ala.org, bannedbooks.world.edu, wikipedia.org

THE WORLDS OF **CLOUD ATLAS**

David Mitchell's acclaimed 2004 novel takes the reader through six different stories that occur in different times, places and even worlds. The first five stories build to the middle section of the story and then each in turn unfold as the book draws to a close. Here's how all are linked.

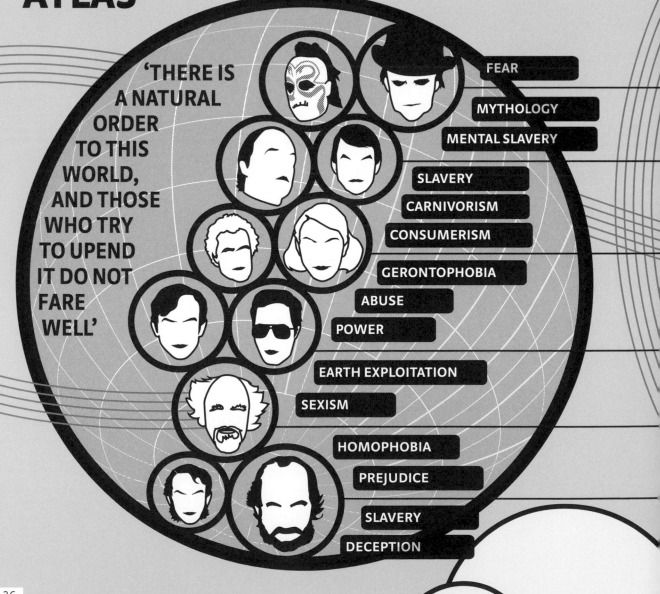

'THERE IS A NATURAL ORDER TO THIS WORLD, AND THOSE WHO TRY TO UPEND IT DO NOT FARE WELL'

FEAR

MYTHOLOGY

MENTAL SLAVERY

SLAVERY

CARNIVORISM

CONSUMERISM

GERONTOPHOBIA

ABUSE

POWER

EARTH EXPLOITATION

SEXISM

HOMOPHOBIA

PREJUDICE

SLAVERY

DECEPTION

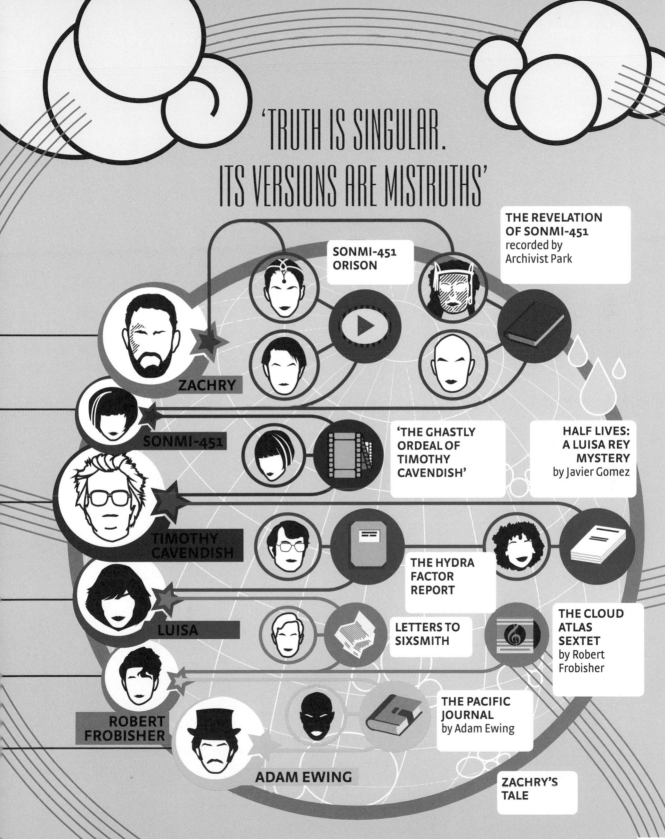

'TRUTH IS SINGULAR.
ITS VERSIONS ARE MISTRUTHS'

THE REVELATION
OF SONMI-451
recorded by
Archivist Park

SONMI-451
ORISON

ZACHRY

SONMI-451

'THE GHASTLY
ORDEAL OF
TIMOTHY
CAVENDISH'

HALF LIVES:
A LUISA REY
MYSTERY
by Javier Gomez

TIMOTHY
CAVENDISH

THE HYDRA
FACTOR
REPORT

THE CLOUD
ATLAS
SEXTET
by Robert
Frobisher

LUISA

LETTERS TO
SIXSMITH

ROBERT
FROBISHER

THE PACIFIC
JOURNAL
by Adam Ewing

ADAM EWING

ZACHRY'S
TALE

WAR AND PEACE

Prince
Nikolai Bolkonsky

Andrei

Natasha

Mitya
(Dimitriy)

Lisa
Karlovna
Bolkonskaya
née Meinena

$+$
Prince Andrei
Nikolayevich
Bolkonsky

Princess
Marya
Bolkonskaya
$+$
Count
Nicolai
Rostov

Sonya (surname
unknown)

Petya
Rostova

Vera
Rostova
$+$
Alphonse
Karlovich Berg

Late
Princess
Bolkonskaya
$+$

Old Prince
Nikolai
Bolkonsky

Alexander
(surname
unknown)

Old Count
Ilya
Rostov
$+$

Old Countess
Natalya
Rostova

Count Pyotr
Nikolaitch
Shinshin

Pyotr's
married
brother
$+$
Pyotr's
cousin

Andrei Rostov's
brother or sister

Andrei
Rostov

Count
Shinshin

Nikolai
Shinshin

Nikolai Shinshin's
brother or sister

Count
Rostov

Count
Shinshin

BOLKONSKY
FAMILY

ROSTOV
FAMILY

SHINSHIN
FAMILY

38

Tolstoy's enormous novel was first published in 1869 in a first edition that ran to 1,225 pages. It has since become the most admired, if least-read, popular book of all time. Here's a handy guide to the family trees of the seven families around whom the plot turns for you to refer to.

Meshenka (Marya) Bezukhova

Liza Bezukhova

Petya Bezukova

name unknown

Princess Anna Drubetskaya

 Natasha Rostova } + { Pierre Bezukhov } + { Hélène Kuragina

 Hippolyte Kuragina

 Anatole Kuragin

 Prince Boris Drubetskoy

Princess Katishe Mamontova

Sophia Mamontova

Olga Mamontova

relationship unknown, either sister or cousin

Prince Semen Mamontov

Princess Mamontova, née Bezukhova

Pierre's mother

Count Kirill Bezukhov

Aline Old Princess Kuragina, née Bezhukhova

Prince Vasili Kuragin

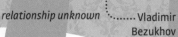

relationship unknown ·······Vladimir Bezukhov

MAMONTOV FAMILY

BEZUKHOV FAMILY

KURAGIN FAMILY

DRUBETSKOY FAMILY

Albert Camus
The Stranger
(novel, 1942)

Paul Bowles
The Sheltering Sky
(novel, 1949)

Fyodor Dostoyevsky
House Of The Dead
(novel, 1861)

Chuck Palahniuk
Fight Club
(novel, 1996)

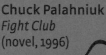

Franz Kafka
The Trial
(novel, 1925)

Abert Camus
Myth Of Sisyphus
(essay, 1942)

EXISTENTIAL SYMBOLS

The great existential writers of the world used symbolic objects in their work to demonstrate aspects of the absurd, nihilism, despair and alienation. This visual guide explains who used what, when and what they represent.

Samuel Beckett
Waiting For Godot
(play, 1953)

Kurt Vonnegut
Slaughterhouse-Five
(novel, 1969)

Albert Camus
Caligula
(play, 1939)

Kobo Abe
The Woman In The Dunes
(novel, 1962)

Paul Celan
Poppy And Memory
(poem, 1952)

Samuel Beckett
Endgame
(play, 1957)

Franz Kafka
The Metamorphosis
(novella, 1915)

Joseph Conrad
Heart Of Darkness
(novel, 1899)

Fyodor Dostoyevsky
Crime And Punishment
(novel, 1866)

Jean-Paul Sartre
Nausea
(novel, 1938)

Ivan Turgenev
Fathers And Sons
(novel, 1862)

Eugène Ionesco
Rhinoceros
(play, 1959)

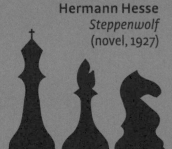

Eugène Ionesco
The New Tenant
(play, 1955)

T.S. Eliot
The Hollow Men
(poem, 1925)

Jean-Paul Sartre
No Exit
(play, 1944)

Hermann Hesse
Steppenwolf
(novel, 1927)

William Faulkner
As I Lay Dying
(novel, 1930)

Edward Albee
*Who's Afraid Of
Virginia Woolf?*
(play, 1962)

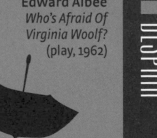

Tom Stoppard
*Rosencrantz And
Guildenstern Are Dead*
(play, 1966)

William Shakespeare
Hamlet
(play, 1599–1602)

Ralph Ellison
Invisible Man
(novel, 1952)

SHAKESPEARE **ETERNAL**

The plays of William Shakespeare have proven to be the inspiration, starting point and whole context for countless rewrites. These six plays have inspired a strange bunch of versions in different modern publishing genres.

HAMLET

2006	2011	2008	1966	2013	2000
Ophelia	*Falling For Hamlet*	*In The Halls Of Elsinore*	*Rosencrantz And Guildenstern Are Dead*	*To Be Or Not To Be: A Chooseable-Path Adventure*	*Gertrude And Claudius*
Lisa M. Klein	Michelle Ray	Brad C. Holson	Tom Stoppard	Ryan North	John Updike

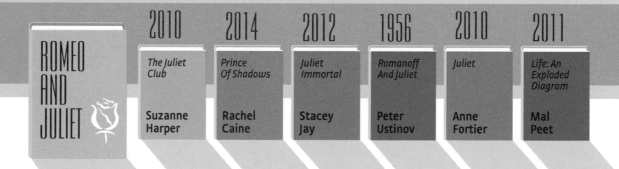

ROMEO AND JULIET

2010	2014	2012	1956	2010	2011
The Juliet Club	*Prince Of Shadows*	*Juliet Immortal*	*Romanoff And Juliet*	*Juliet*	*Life: An Exploded Diagram*
Suzanne Harper	Rachel Caine	Stacey Jay	Peter Ustinov	Anne Fortier	Mal Peet

A MIDSUMMER NIGHT'S DREAM

2004	2013	1988	1992	1997	2011
This Must Be Love	*Midsummer Magic*	*Faerie Tale*	*Lords And Ladies (Discworld)*	*A Midsummer Night's Dream*	*The Great Night*
Tui Sutherland	Julia Williams	Raymond E. Feist	Terry Pratchett	Andrew Harman	Chris Adrian

YOUNG ADULT	CHICK-LIT	HORROR	COMEDY	ACTION/ADVENTURE	LITERARY FICTION

THE TEMPEST

2013	2010	2010	2012	2010	1989
Undine	*The Gentleman Poet*	*Prospero Lost*	*Tempestuous (Twisted Lit)*	*The Dream Of Perpetual Motion*	*Mama Day*
Penni Russon	Kathryn Johnson	L. Jagi Lamplighter	Askew & Helmes	Dexter Palmer	Gloria Naylor

MACBETH

2007	2008	2008	1980	1982	1973
Enter Three Witches	*Lady MacBeth: A Novel*	*The Lost Kings*	*Wyrd Sisters (Discworld)*	*Light Thickens*	*Macbett*
Caroline B. Cooney	Susan Fraser King	Andrew Reimann	Terry Pratchett	Naigo Marsh	Eugene Ionesco

THE MERCHANT OF VENICE

2001	2004	2008	2014	2003	1994
Shylock's Daughter	*Shylock's Daughter: A Novel Of Love In Venice*	*The Merchant Of Venice*	*The Serpent Of Venice: A Novel*	*The Merchant Of Vengeance*	*Operation Shylock: A Confession*
Mirjam Pressler	Erica Jong	Gareth Hinds	Christopher Moore	Simon Hawke	Philip Roth

THE SHAPES OF STORIES ACCORDING TO
KURT VONNEGUT

MAN IN HOLE

The main character gets into trouble, then gets out of it again, and ends up better off for the experience.

 Arsenic and Old Lace

 Harold & Kumar Go To White Castle

BOY MEETS GIRL

The main character comes across something wonderful, gets it, loses it, then gets it back forever.

 Jane Eyre

 Eternal Sunshine Of The Spotless Mind

FROM BAD TO WORSE

The main character starts off poorly then gets continually worse with no hope for improvement.

 The Metamorphosis

 The Twilight Zone

WHICH WAY IS UP?

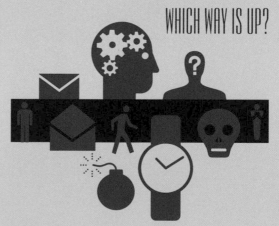

The story has a lifelike ambiguity that keeps us from knowing if new developments are good or bad.

 Hamlet

 The Sopranos

Kurt Vonnegut gained worldwide fame and adoration through the publication of his novels, including Slaughterhouse-Five, Cat's Cradle, Breakfast Of Champions, *and more. But it was his rejected master's thesis in anthropology that he called his prettiest contribution to culture. The basic idea of his thesis was that a story's main character has ups and downs that can be graphed to reveal the story's shape. The shape of a society's stories, he said, is at least as interesting as the shape of its pots or spearheads. Let's have a look.*

CREATION STORY

In many cultures' creation stories, humankind receives incremental gifts from a deity. First, major staples like the earth and sky, then smaller things like sparrows and cell phones. Not a common shape for Western stories, however.

OLD TESTAMENT

Humankind receives incremental gifts from a deity, but is suddenly ousted from good standing in a fall of enormous proportions.

 Great Expectations with original ending

NEW TESTAMENT

Humankind receives incremental gifts from a deity, is suddenly ousted from good standing, but then receives off-the-charts bliss.

 Great Expectations with revised ending

CINDERELLA

It was the similarity between the shapes of *Cinderella* and the New Testament that thrilled Vonnegut for the first time in 1947, and then over the course of his life as he continued to write essays and give lectures on the shapes of stories.

A Man Without A Country and *Palm Sunday* by Kurt Vonnegut

REFERENCES **REQUIRED**

Writers are often inspired by other writers. If it's not Shakespeare then it's usually another great from the canon of literary history. However, there are now works of fiction that are considered a part of the canon that were inspired by earlier, lesser-known works.

NEW WORK

Vanity Fair novel by William Makepeace Thackeray — **1847**

Far From The Madding Crowd novel by Thomas Hardy — **1874**

A Passage To India novel by E.M. Forster — **1924**

As I Lay Dying novel by William Faulkner — **1930**

Tender Is the Night novel by F. Scott Fitzgerald — **1932**

Of Mice And Men novella by John Steinbeck — **1937**

Blithe Spirit play by Noël Coward — **1941**

Things Fall Apart novel by Chinua Achebe — **1958**

Mother Night novel by Kurt Vonnegut — **1961**

I Know Why The Caged Bird Sings autobiography by Maya Angelou — **1969**

A Confederacy Of Dunces novel by John Kennedy Toole — **1980**

His Dark Materials trilogy by Philip Pullman — **1995–2000**

Everything Is Illuminated novel by Jonathan Safran Foer — **2002**

The Curious Incident Of The Dog In The Night-Time novel by Mark Haddon — **2003**

No Country For Old Men novel by Cormac McCarthy — **2005**

c.7–8th century – *The Odyssey* epic poem by Homer

1667 – *Paradise Lost* epic poem by John Milton

1678 – *The Pilgrim's Progress* work by John Bunyan

1703 – *Thoughts On Various Subjects, Moral And Diverting* essay by Jonathan Swift

1751 – *Elegy Written In A Country Churchyard* poem by Thomas Gray

1785 – *To A Mouse* poem by Robert Burns

1808 – *Faust Part One* play by Johann Wolfgang von Goethe

1819 – *Ode To A Nightingale* poem by John Keats

1820 – *To A Skylark* poem by Percy Bysshe Shelley

1855 – Walt Whitman's poem of the same name

1892 – *Silver Blaze* Sherlock Holmes story by Arthur Conan Doyle

1899 – *Sympathy* poem by Paul Laurence Dunbar

1919 – *The Second Coming* poem by W.B. Yeats

1926 – *Sailing To Byzantium* poem by W.B. Yeats

1984 – *The Unbearable Lightness Of Being* novel by Milan Kundera

THE BLOOMSBURY
GROUP NETWORK

They were the most infamous, ingenious and interrelated group of writers, critics, artists and publishers in London in the early 20th century, and helped define and promote modernism in literature. Here's who they were, what they did, and with whom.

Clive Bell
Art Critic

Vanessa Bell
Post-Impressionist Painter

E.M. Forster
Novelist

Roger Fry
Art Critic and
Post-Impressionist Painter

Duncan Grant
Post-Impressionist
Painter

Roger Fry, Vanessa Bell and Duncan Grant collaborated
on the Omega Workshops design enterprise

Vanessa Bell painted portraits of Virginia Woolf and David Garnett

Quentin Bell wrote biography of Virginia Woolf

Vita Sackville-West
Novelist

David Garnett
Writer and Publisher

Angelica Garnett
Writer and Painter

daughter of Vanessa Bell and
Duncan Grant (raised as Clive Bell's)

sons of Vanessa Bell and Clive Bell

Quentin Bell
Art Historian and Author

Julian Bell
Poet

48

Studied together at Cambridge · Siblings · Cousins · Lovers

Marriages · Parents/Children · Artistic collaborations

John Maynard Keynes
Economist

Desmond MacCarthy
Literary Journalist

Lytton Strachey
Biographer

James Strachey
Psychoanalyst

Leonard Woolf
Essayist and Novelist

Leonard Woolf and Virginia Woolf founded the Hogarth Press, which published works by Virginia Woolf, Vanessa Bell and Vita Sackville-West

Virginia Woolf wrote biography of Roger Fry

Mary (Molly) MacCarthy
Novelist

Saxon Sydney-Turner
Civil Servant

Karin Stephen
Psychoanalyst and Psychologist

Adrian Stephen
Author and Psychoanalyst

Virginia Woolf
Novelist

WRITER'S REST

Here are the sleeping and writing patterns of more than a dozen of the world's most famous authors.

hours writing

HOURS SPENT WRITING

Jane Austen (1775–1817)	5
Anthony Trollope (1815–1882)	3
Jean-Paul Sartre (1905–1980)	6
Simone de Beauvoir (1908–1986)	7
Saul Bellow (1915–2005)	4
Kingsley Amis (1922–1995)	9

Maya Angelou (1928–2014)	7
John Updike (1932–2009)	3.5
Philip Roth (1933–2018)	8
Joyce Carol Oates (1938–)	8
Stephen King (1947–)	4
David Foster Wallace (1962–2008)	3

HOURS SPENT WRITING/SLEEPING

	✎	☾		✎	☾
Honoré de Balzac (1799–1850)	13.5	7.5	Vladimir Nabokov (1899–1977)	11.5	10
Charles Dickens (1812–1870)	5	7	Georges Simenon (1903–1989)	3	8
Gustave Flaubert (1821–1880)	5	7	W.H. Auden (1907–1973)	8.5	8.5
Gertrude Stein (1874–1946)	0.5	7	Flannery O'Connor (1925–1964)	3	9
Thomas Mann (1875–1955)	3	8	William Styron (1925–2006)	4	9
Franz Kafka (1883–1924)	3	8.5	Haruki Murakami (1949–)	5	7
F. Scott Fitzgerald (1896–1940)	10.5	7			

Daily Rituals: How Great Minds Make Time, Find Inspiration, and Get to Work by Mason Currey (Picador, 2013)   51

IN THE LAP OF **THE GODS**

The works of Homer, Hesiod, Sophocles and other ancient Greek writers are filled with the names and deeds of the gods who ruled the world. This is a who's who of the first tier of Greek gods and goddesses, their symbols, patronage and family tree.

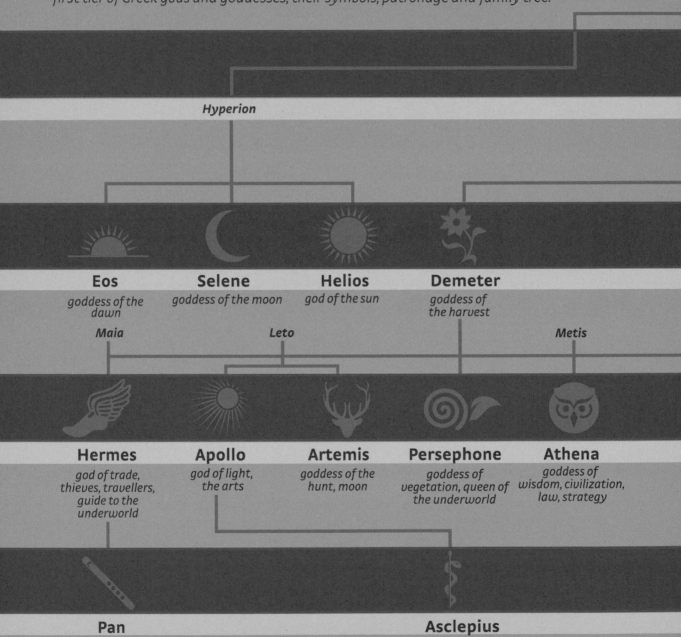

Hyperion

Eos
goddess of the dawn

Selene
goddess of the moon

Helios
god of the sun

Demeter
goddess of the harvest

Maia

Leto

Metis

Hermes
god of trade, thieves, travellers, guide to the underworld

Apollo
god of light, the arts

Artemis
goddess of the hunt, moon

Persephone
goddess of vegetation, queen of the underworld

Athena
goddess of wisdom, civilization, law, strategy

Pan
god of nature, the wild, woods, shepherds, fields

Asclepius
god of medicine, health

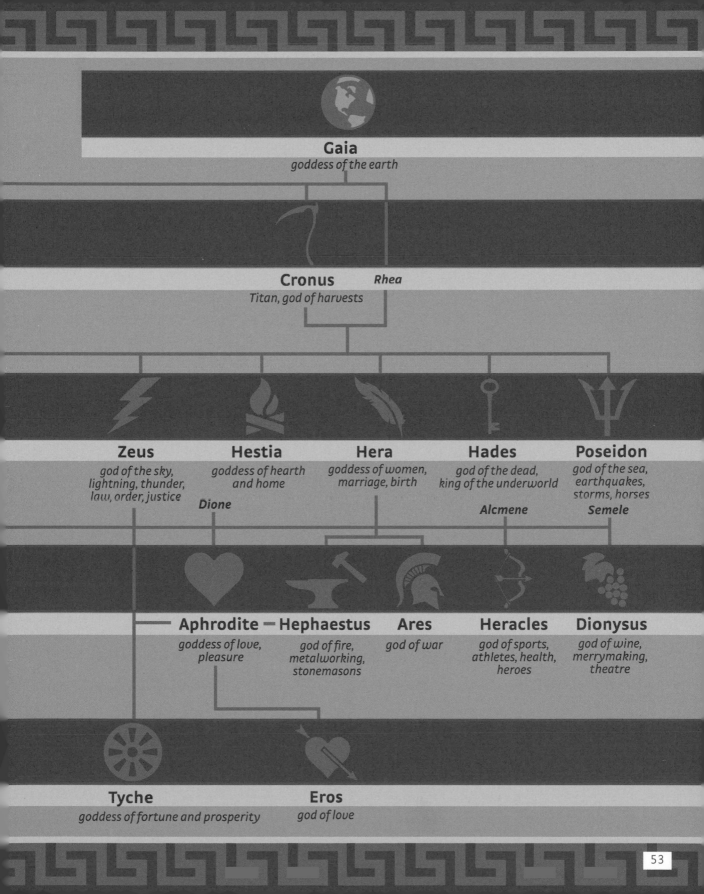

Gaia
goddess of the earth

Cronus — *Rhea*
Titan, god of harvests

Zeus
god of the sky, lightning, thunder, law, order, justice
Dione

Hestia
goddess of hearth and home

Hera
goddess of women, marriage, birth

Hades
god of the dead, king of the underworld
Alcmene

Poseidon
god of the sea, earthquakes, storms, horses
Semele

Aphrodite — **Hephaestus**
goddess of love, pleasure
god of fire, metalworking, stonemasons

Ares
god of war

Heracles
god of sports, athletes, health, heroes

Dionysus
god of wine, merrymaking, theatre

Tyche
goddess of fortune and prosperity

Eros
god of love

DUCK **OR** SEAGULL?

The social dramas of Norwegian playwright Henrik Ibsen (1828–1906) and Russian Anton Chekhov (1860–1904) changed the shape and concerns of theatre in the 20th century. Their works had a lot in common, as this examination of four of the best known and most popular plays by each man demonstrates.

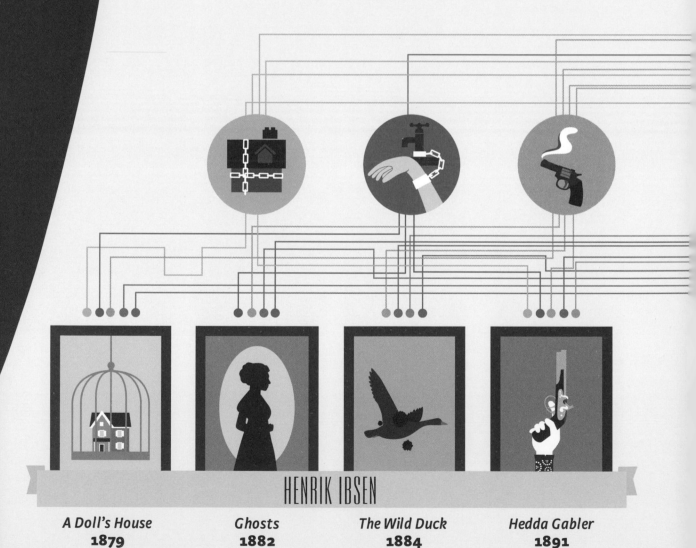

HENRIK IBSEN

A Doll's House	*Ghosts*	*The Wild Duck*	*Hedda Gabler*
1879	**1882**	**1884**	**1891**

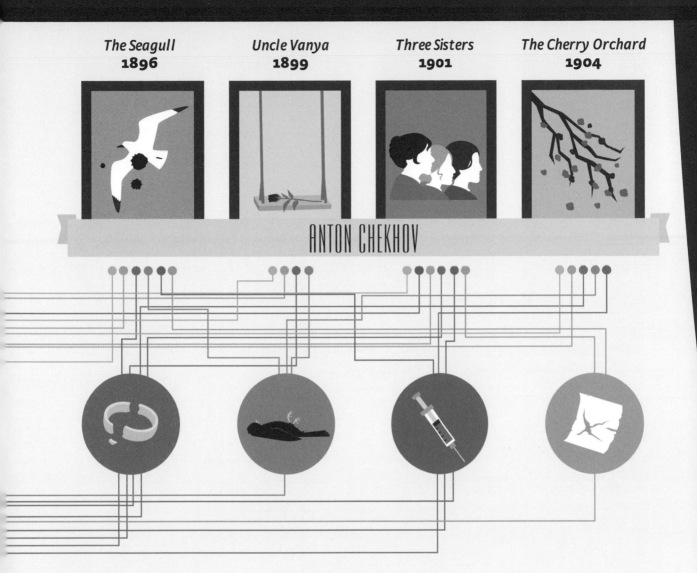

The Seagull
1896

Uncle Vanya
1899

Three Sisters
1901

The Cherry Orchard
1904

ANTON CHEKHOV

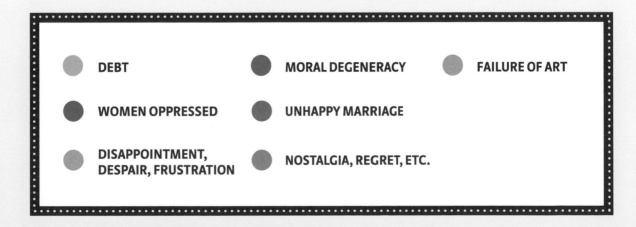

- DEBT
- MORAL DEGENERACY
- FAILURE OF ART
- WOMEN OPPRESSED
- UNHAPPY MARRIAGE
- DISAPPOINTMENT, DESPAIR, FRUSTRATION
- NOSTALGIA, REGRET, ETC.

MEET ME IN **PARIS**

Imagining the literary characters of different centuries and authors meeting at the great locations of Paris where their stories are set.

H Hotel Ritz, Place Vendôme
Head waiter meets bartender

Aime from Marcel Proust's *In Search Of Lost Time*
meets
Alix from F. Scott Fitzgerald's *Babylon Revisited*

K   Arc de Triomphe
Idealistic nobleman meets misanthropic nobleman

D'Artagnan from Alexandre Dumas's *The Three Musketeers*
meets
Alceste from Molière's *The Misanthrope*

B   The Right Bank, Palais Royale
Traitorous poet meets gullible businessman

Lucien de Rubempré from Honoré de Balzac's *Lost Illusions*
meets
Christopher Newman from Henry James's *The American*

C   Left Bank, the Latin Quarter
Impotent journalist meets runaway stockbroker

Jake Barnes from Ernest Hemingway's *The Sun Also Rises*
meets
Charles Strickland from Somerset Maugham's *The Moon And Sixpence*

G   Boulevard Saint-Germaine, Café Flor
Existentialist meets individual

Mathieu from Jean-Paul Sartre's *The Age Of Reason*
meets
Jean from Simone de Beauvoir's *Blood Of Others*

F   Sorbonne District
Bored law student meets unstable middle-aged housewife

Dominique from Françoise Sagan's *A Certain Smile*
meets
Sasha Jensen from Jean Rhys's *Good Morning Midnight*

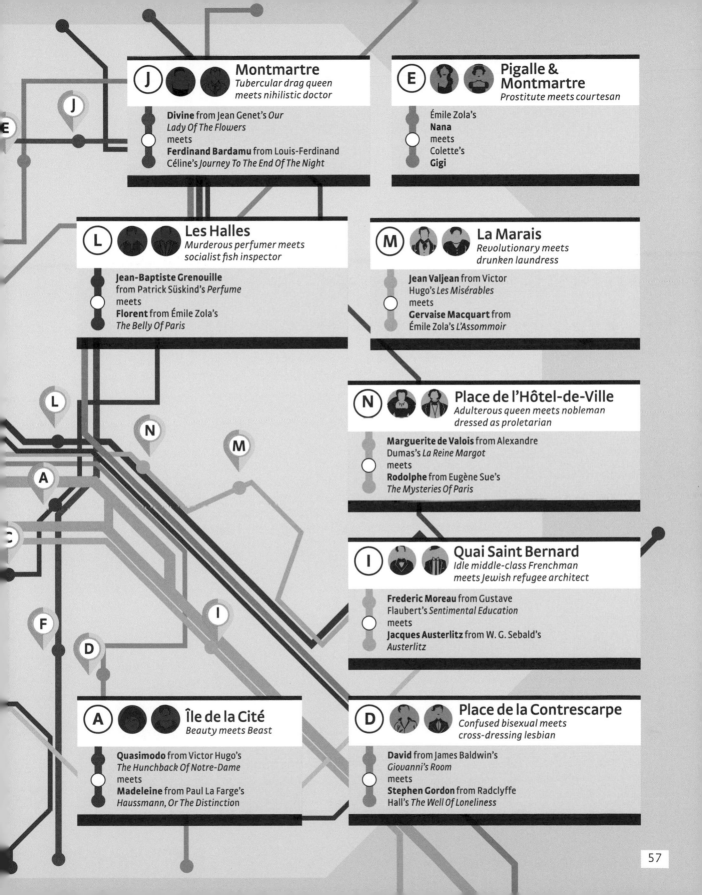

J Montmartre
Tubercular drag queen meets nihilistic doctor

Divine from Jean Genet's *Our Lady Of The Flowers*
meets
Ferdinand Bardamu from Louis-Ferdinand Céline's *Journey To The End Of The Night*

E Pigalle & Montmartre
Prostitute meets courtesan

Émile Zola's **Nana**
meets
Colette's **Gigi**

L Les Halles
Murderous perfumer meets socialist fish inspector

Jean-Baptiste Grenouille from Patrick Süskind's *Perfume*
meets
Florent from Émile Zola's *The Belly Of Paris*

M La Marais
Revolutionary meets drunken laundress

Jean Valjean from Victor Hugo's *Les Misérables*
meets
Gervaise Macquart from Émile Zola's *L'Assommoir*

N Place de l'Hôtel-de-Ville
Adulterous queen meets nobleman dressed as proletarian

Marguerite de Valois from Alexandre Dumas's *La Reine Margot*
meets
Rodolphe from Eugène Sue's *The Mysteries Of Paris*

I Quai Saint Bernard
Idle middle-class Frenchman meets Jewish refugee architect

Frederic Moreau from Gustave Flaubert's *Sentimental Education*
meets
Jacques Austerlitz from W. G. Sebald's *Austerlitz*

A Île de la Cité
Beauty meets Beast

Quasimodo from Victor Hugo's *The Hunchback Of Notre-Dame*
meets
Madeleine from Paul La Farge's *Haussmann, Or The Distinction*

D Place de la Contrescarpe
Confused bisexual meets cross-dressing lesbian

David from James Baldwin's *Giovanni's Room*
meets
Stephen Gordon from Radclyffe Hall's *The Well Of Loneliness*

THE **FINAL** CHAPTER

In death, as so often in life, truth is stranger than fiction. And it is predominantly novelists, poets and playwrights who have met with sad and terrible deaths, as these famous examples from around the world show.

 Suicide

 Death stranger than fiction

 Murder

ALBERT CAMUS
novelist
{ d. 4 January 1960, Villeblevin, Burgundy, France }

Car crashed into a tree on a straight road on a bright day, no other vehicles involved. Aged 46.

JOHN KENNEDY TOOLE
novelist
{ d. 26 March 1969, Biloxi, MS }

Gassed by car exhaust fumes. Aged 31.

DONALD GOINES
(aka Al C. Clark)
novelist
{ d. 21 October 1974, Detroit, MI }

Gunshot wounds, unknown assailant. Aged 37.

ROLAND BARTHES
literary critic
d. 25 February 1980, Paris, France

Hit by a laundry van while crossing the road. Aged 64.

BRUNO SCHULZ
novelist
{ d. 19 November 1942, Drohobych, Ukraine }

Shot by Gestapo officer. Aged 50.

MARGARET MITCHELL
novelist
{ d. 11 August 1949, Atlanta, GA }

Drunk driver accident. Aged 48.

SYLVIA PLATH
poet
{ d. 11 February 1963, London, England }

Gassed in her own oven. Aged 30.

EDGAR ALLAN POE
poet, novelist
{ d. 7 October 1849, Baltimore, MD }

Found in the street semi-conscious and dressed in clothes that weren't his. Medical records have been lost. Aged 40.

HART CRANE
poet
{ d. 27 April 1932, Gulf of Florida }

Drowned. Aged 32.

CHRISTOPHER MARLOWE
playwright
{ d. 30 May 1593, London, England }

Stabbed. Aged 29.

DAN ANDERSSON
poet, critic
{ d. 16 September 1920, Stockholm, Sweden }

Hydrogen cyanide poisoning from bedbug extermination procedure. Aged 32.

GEORGI MARKOV

novelist, playwright
{ d. 11 September 1978,
London, England }

Ricin poisoning by
Bulgarian secret
service. Aged 49.

LEICESTER HEMINGWAY

non-fiction writer
{ d. 13 September 1982,
Miami Beach, FL }

Gunshot to the
head. Aged 67.

JOY ADAMSON

memoirist
{ d. 3 January 1980, Shaba
National Reserve, Kenya }

Hacked to death with
a machete by ex-
employee. Aged 69.

YUKIO MISHIMA

playwright, poet
{ d. 25 November,
1970, Tokyo, Japan }

Self-disembowelment.
Aged 45.

PIER PAOLO PASOLINI

poet
{ d. 2 November
1975, Ostia, Italy }

Repeatedly run over
with his own car by a
prostitute. Aged 53.

TENNESSEE WILLIAMS

playwright
{ d. 24 February 1983,
New York, NY }

Choked to death on
a medicine bottle
cap. Aged 71.

B.S. JOHNSON

novelist, poet
{ d. 13 November 1973,
London, England }

Slit wrists. Aged 40.

MAXWELL BODENHEIM

poet
{ d. 6 February 1954,
New York, NY }

Shot twice by
hobo. Aged 62.

ERNEST HEMINGWAY

novelist
{ d. 2 July 1961,
Ketchum, ID }

Gunshot to the
head. Aged 61.

RANDALL JARRELL

poet, critic
{ d. 14 October 1965,
Chapel Hill, NC }

Hit by car on
highway. Aged 51.

JOE ORTON

playwright
{ d. 9 August 1967,
London, England }

Bludgeoned with
a hammer by lover
Kenneth Halliwell.
Aged 34.

VIRGINIA WOOLF

novelist
{ d. 28 March 1941,
River Ouse,
Rodmell, England }

Drowned. Aged 59.

FEDERICO GARCIA LORCA

playwright
{ d. 19 August 1936,
Granada }

Stabbed above the eye
in a bar fight, unknown
assailant. Aged 29.

ZELDA FITZGERALD

novelist
{ d. 10 March 1948,
Asheville, NC }

Burned in a fire at
sanatorium. Aged 47.

STEFAN ZWEIG

novelist, playwright
{ d. 22 February 1942,
Rio de Janeiro, Brazil }

Barbiturate
overdose. Aged 60.

REMEMBRANCE	23%
MADELEINES	15%
TIME	10%
ART	9%
SOCIAL CLIMBING	7%
MOTHER	7%
HOMOSEXUALITY	7%
WRITER'S BLOCK	6%
MEALS	6%
THEATRE	4%
TAILORS	3%
CONFLICT	2%
SLEEP	1%

WHAT WAS ON **MARCEL PROUST**'S MIND?

Marcel Proust (1871–1922) is most famous for writing the seven-volume In Search Of Lost Time, *and for its inspiration being a bite of a little French fancy, dipped in tea. Written over the course of the last 13 years of his life, Proust's masterwork is filled with detail of memory, reflections on perception, aspects of social interaction and contemporary French society. From it we can deduce that this is mostly what was on his mind.*

FELINE **FEELINGS**

Novelists love cats, as much for their capacity to embody malevolence as for cuteness and faithfulness. Here is a literary cat matrix with the famous felines of imagination plotted on it.

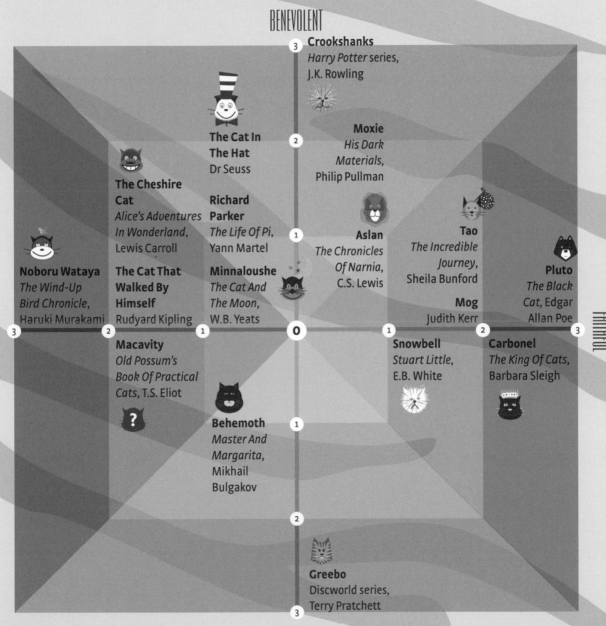

BENEVOLENT

3 **Crookshanks**
Harry Potter series,
J.K. Rowling

2 **Moxie**
His Dark Materials,
Philip Pullman

The Cat In The Hat
Dr Seuss

The Cheshire Cat
Alice's Adventures In Wonderland,
Lewis Carroll

Richard Parker
The Life Of Pi,
Yann Martel

Tao
The Incredible Journey,
Sheila Bunford

1 **Aslan**
The Chronicles Of Narnia,
C.S. Lewis

Noboru Wataya
The Wind-Up Bird Chronicle,
Haruki Murakami

The Cat That Walked By Himself
Rudyard Kipling

Minnaloushe
The Cat And The Moon,
W.B. Yeats

Mog
Judith Kerr

Pluto
The Black Cat, Edgar Allan Poe

ELUSIVE 3 ⎯ 2 ⎯ 1 ⎯ **0** ⎯ 1 ⎯ 2 ⎯ 3 **FAITHFUL**

Macavity
Old Possum's Book Of Practical Cats, T.S. Eliot

Snowbell
Stuart Little,
E.B. White

Carbonel
The King Of Cats,
Barbara Sleigh

1 **Behemoth**
Master And Margarita,
Mikhail Bulgakov

2

Greebo
Discworld series,
Terry Pratchett

3

MALEVOLENT

LINES OF INFLUENCE:
SHAKESPEARE

Before Shakespeare, there were poets and playwrights that he read and was inspired by. During his lifetime he worked with other playwrights, and read essayists and poets for inspiration. In the two centuries after his death, poets, playwrights, essayists and critics used his work, some of them earning the reputation as the 'Shakespeare' of their homeland. Tracing his lines of influence from 70 BCE to the 19th century.

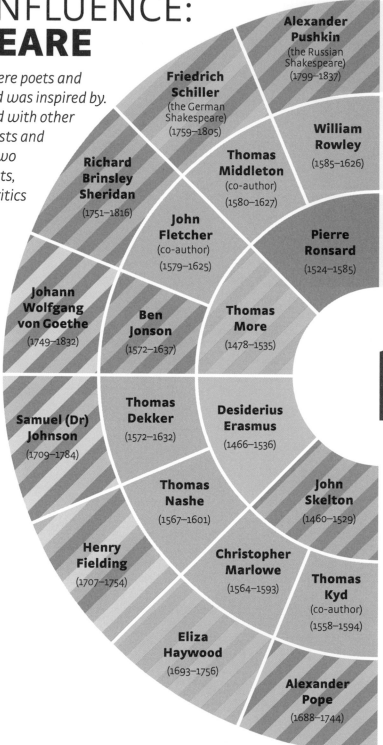

Alexander Pushkin
(the Russian Shakespeare)
(1799–1837)

Friedrich Schiller
(the German Shakespeare)
(1759–1805)

William Rowley
(1585–1626)

Richard Brinsley Sheridan
(1751–1816)

Thomas Middleton
(co-author)
(1580–1627)

John Fletcher
(co-author)
(1579–1625)

Pierre Ronsard
(1524–1585)

Johann Wolfgang von Goethe
(1749–1832)

Ben Jonson
(1572–1637)

Thomas More
(1478–1535)

Samuel (Dr) Johnson
(1709–1784)

Thomas Dekker
(1572–1632)

Desiderius Erasmus
(1466–1536)

John Skelton
(1460–1529)

Thomas Nashe
(1567–1601)

Henry Fielding
(1707–1754)

Christopher Marlowe
(1564–1593)

Thomas Kyd
(co-author)
(1558–1594)

Eliza Haywood
(1693–1756)

Alexander Pope
(1688–1744)

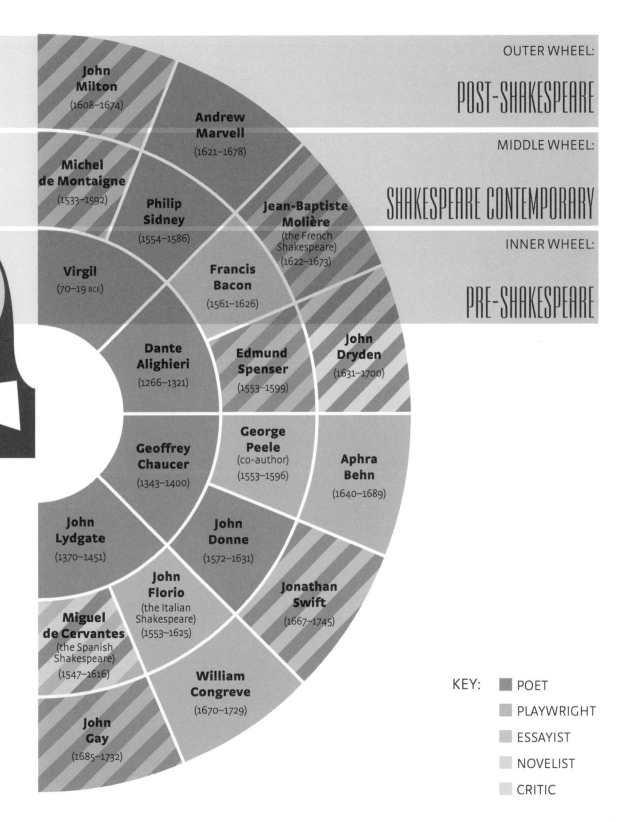

OUTER WHEEL:

POST-SHAKESPEARE

MIDDLE WHEEL:

SHAKESPEARE CONTEMPORARY

INNER WHEEL:

PRE-SHAKESPEARE

John Milton
(1608–1674)

Andrew Marvell
(1621–1678)

Michel de Montaigne
(1533–1592)

Philip Sidney
(1554–1586)

Jean-Baptiste Molière
(the French Shakespeare)
(1622–1673)

Virgil
(70–19 BCE)

Francis Bacon
(1561–1626)

Dante Alighieri
(1266–1321)

Edmund Spenser
(1553–1599)

John Dryden
(1631–1700)

Geoffrey Chaucer
(1343–1400)

George Peele
(co-author)
(1553–1596)

Aphra Behn
(1640–1689)

John Lydgate
(1370–1451)

John Donne
(1572–1631)

John Florio
(the Italian Shakespeare)
(1553–1625)

Jonathan Swift
(1667–1745)

Miguel de Cervantes
(the Spanish Shakespeare)
(1547–1616)

William Congreve
(1670–1729)

John Gay
(1685–1732)

KEY:
- POET
- PLAYWRIGHT
- ESSAYIST
- NOVELIST
- CRITIC

FUTURE **PAST**

Here are the novelists who have created fictional future worlds in which people interact with technology that was unknown at the time of writing. Some of the predictions can be traced to scientific work being done at the time – Jules Verne had seen sketches for a German submarine three years before writing about the Nautilus, so it isn't included here – others are pure imagination. Until later.

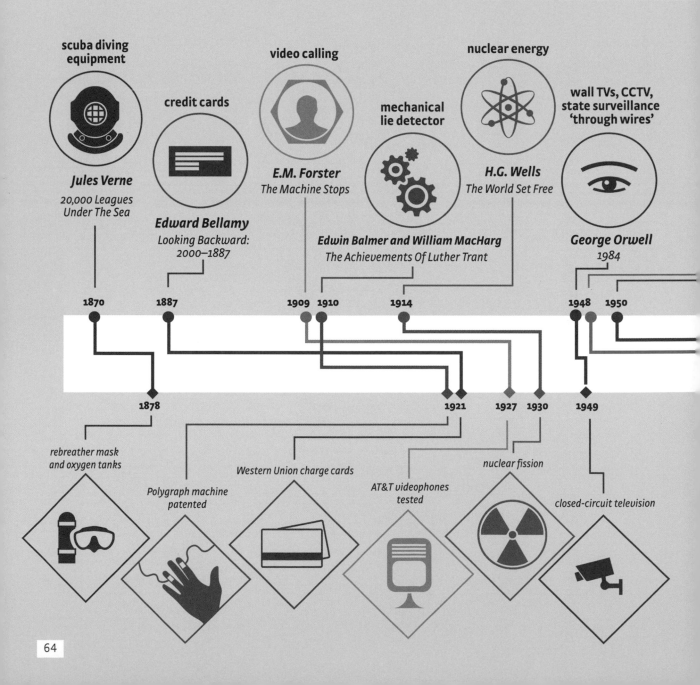

scuba diving equipment

Jules Verne

20,000 Leagues Under The Sea

credit cards

Edward Bellamy

Looking Backward: 2000–1887

video calling

E.M. Forster

The Machine Stops

mechanical lie detector

Edwin Balmer and William MacHarg

The Achievements Of Luther Trant

nuclear energy

H.G. Wells

The World Set Free

wall TVs, CCTV, state surveillance 'through wires'

George Orwell

1984

1870   1887   1909   1910   1914   1948   1950

1878   1921   1927   1930   1949

rebreather mask and oxygen tanks

Polygraph machine patented

Western Union charge cards

AT&T videophones tested

nuclear fission

closed-circuit television

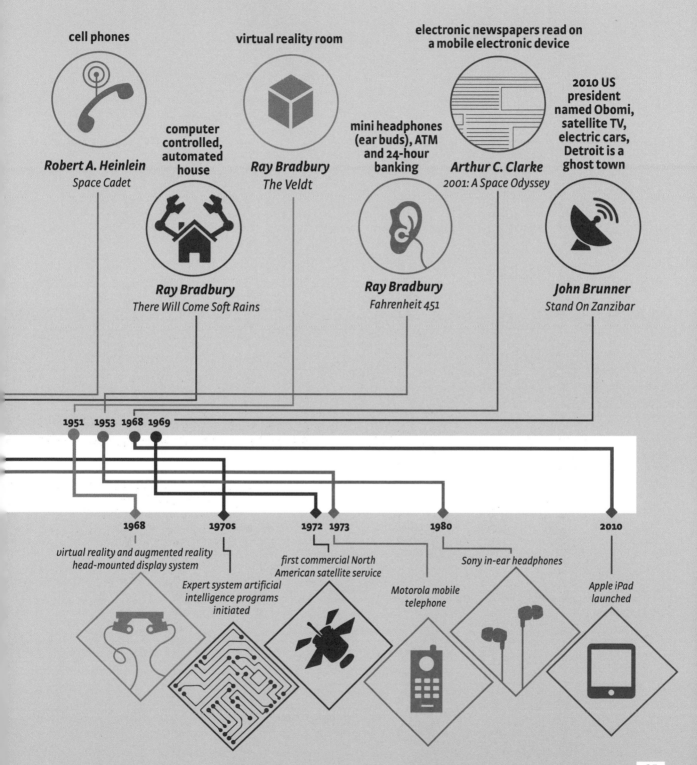

cell phones

Robert A. Heinlein
Space Cadet

computer controlled, automated house

Ray Bradbury
There Will Come Soft Rains

virtual reality room

Ray Bradbury
The Veldt

mini headphones (ear buds), ATM and 24-hour banking

Ray Bradbury
Fahrenheit 451

electronic newspapers read on a mobile electronic device

Arthur C. Clarke
2001: A Space Odyssey

2010 US president named Obomi, satellite TV, electric cars, Detroit is a ghost town

John Brunner
Stand On Zanzibar

1951   1953   1968   1969

1968   1970s   1972   1973   1980   2010

virtual reality and augmented reality head-mounted display system

Expert system artificial intelligence programs initiated

first commercial North American satellite service

Motorola mobile telephone

Sony in-ear headphones

Apple iPad launched

65

LIVING
WRIT LARGE

Joseph Conrad (1857–1924)
Heart Of Darkness (1899), Lord Jim (1900), Typhoon (1902), The Shadow Line (1917)

Mark Twain (1835–1910)
The Adventures Of Tom Sawyer (1876), The Adventures of Huckleberry Finn (1884)

Herman Melville (1819–1891)
Typee (1846), Omoo (1847), Mardi (1849), Moby-Dick (1851)

Jack London (1876–1916)
The Call Of The Wild (1903), White Fang (1906)

George Orwell (1903–1950)
Burmese Days (1934)

Jack London (1876–1916)
The Sea-Wolf (1904)

P.C. Wren (1875–1941)
Beau Geste (1924)

Mark Twain (1835–1910)
Roughing It (1872)

Charles Dickens (1812–1870)
Hard Times (1854)

steamboat pilot (1859–1861)

gold prospector (1897–1899)

merchant seaman (1890–1892)

silver miner (1862)

merchant seaman (1874–1893)

merchant seaman (1839–1844)

policeman (1922–1926)

foreign legion soldier (1917–1922)

blacking factory hand (1824)

'Write what you know' is a cliché of writing courses everywhere, and as these international best-selling authors prove, it's advice that works. All of the authors here translated their civilian work experiences into novels. Some lived more adventurous lives than others, but as Charles Bukowski showed, even working in a post office can be turned into great fiction.

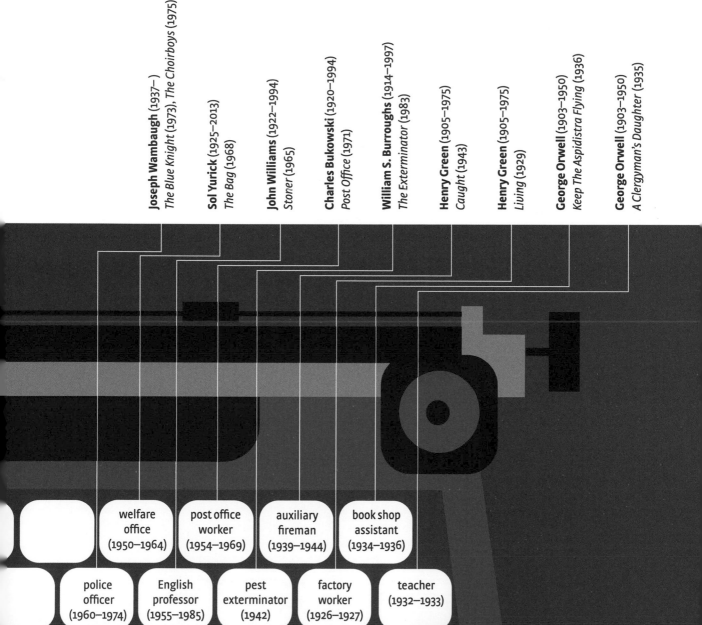

Joseph Wambaugh (1937–)
The Blue Knight (1973), *The Choirboys* (1975)

Sol Yurick (1925–2013)
The Bag (1968)

John Williams (1922–1994)
Stoner (1965)

Charles Bukowski (1920–1994)
Post Office (1971)

William S. Burroughs (1914–1997)
The Exterminator (1983)

Henry Green (1905–1975)
Caught (1943)

Henry Green (1905–1975)
Living (1929)

George Orwell (1903–1950)
Keep The Aspidistra Flying (1936)

George Orwell (1903–1950)
A Clergyman's Daughter (1935)

welfare office (1950–1964)

post office worker (1954–1969)

auxiliary fireman (1939–1944)

book shop assistant (1934–1936)

police officer (1960–1974)

English professor (1955–1985)

pest exterminator (1942)

factory worker (1926–1927)

teacher (1932–1933)

FLOGGING A **DEAD HORSE**

Just because an author dies, it doesn't mean that their characters have to. As well as manuscripts finished but not published before death, there are always sequels, prequels and further adventures of, written in the style of the originals. These 14 famous originals have been extended well beyond the death of their originator.

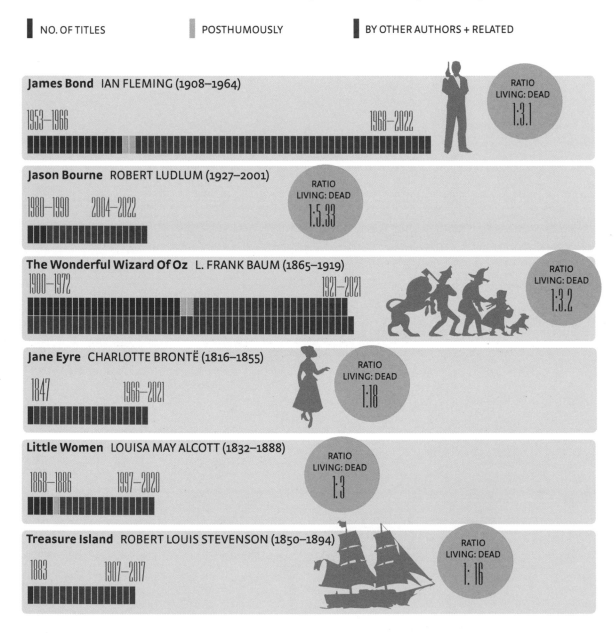

■ NO. OF TITLES ■ POSTHUMOUSLY ■ BY OTHER AUTHORS + RELATED

James Bond IAN FLEMING (1908–1964)
1953–1966 1968–2022
RATIO LIVING: DEAD 1:3.1

Jason Bourne ROBERT LUDLUM (1927–2001)
1980–1990 2004–2022
RATIO LIVING: DEAD 1:5.33

The Wonderful Wizard Of Oz L. FRANK BAUM (1865–1919)
1900–1972 1921–2021
RATIO LIVING: DEAD 1:3.2

Jane Eyre CHARLOTTE BRONTË (1816–1855)
1847 1966–2021
RATIO LIVING: DEAD 1:18

Little Women LOUISA MAY ALCOTT (1832–1888)
1868–1886 1997–2020
RATIO LIVING: DEAD 1:3

Treasure Island ROBERT LOUIS STEVENSON (1850–1894)
1883 1907–2017
RATIO LIVING: DEAD 1:16

Foundation Universe ISAAC ASIMOV (1920–1992)

1950–1993   1989–1999

RATIO
LIVING: DEAD
1: 0.57

Boxcar Children GERTRUDE CHANDLER WARNER (1890–1979)

1924–1979   1991–2022

RATIO
LIVING: DEAD
1: 10.26

Dune FRANK HERBERT (1920–1986)

1965–1985   1984–2022

RATIO
LIVING: DEAD
1: 2.67

Little House On the Prairie LAURA INGALLS WILDER (1867–1957)

1932–2006   1992–2012

RATIO
LIVING: DEAD
1: 2.33

Wuthering Heights EMILY BRONTË (1818–1848)

1847   1977–2016

RATIO
LIVING: DEAD
1: 10

Great Expectations CHARLES DICKENS (1812–1870)

1861   1997–2013

RATIO
LIVING: DEAD
1: 5

The Wind In The Willows KENNETH GRAHAME (1859–1932)

1908   1981–2019

RATIO
LIVING: DEAD
1: 10

Madame Bovary GUSTAVE FLAUBERT (1821–1880)

1856   1864–2011

RATIO
LIVING: DEAD
1: 2

Lewis Carroll	Through The Looking Glass	1871
L. Frank Baum	The Wonderful Wizard Of Oz	1900
J.M. Barrie	Peter Pan	1911
Frances Hodgson Burnett	The Secret Garden	1911
C.S. Lewis	The Lion, The Witch And The Wardrobe	1950
Philippa Pearce	Tom's Midnight Garden	1958
Norton Juster	The Phantom Tollbooth	1961
Pierre Berton	The Secret World Of Og	1961
Madeleine L'Engle	A Wrinkle In Time	1962
Maurice Sendak	Where The Wild Things Are	1963
Clive King	Stig Of The Dump	1963
Roald Dahl	Charlie And The Chocolate Factory	1964
Michael Ende	The Neverending Story	1983
Eva Ibbotson	The Secret Of Platform 13	1994
Enid Blyton	Faraway Tree series	1939–1951
David McKee	Mr Benn series	1967–
Philip Pullman	His Dark Materials trilogy	1995–2000
J.K. Rowling	Harry Potter series	1997–2007
Cornelia Funke	Inkheart trilogy	2003–2007

PORTAL TO **ANOTHER WORLD**

Good books offer the reader a window to another world, and good children's books transport their reader (or listener) into different worlds. Especially those in which a seemingly ordinary object turns out to be a doorway to a parallel universe for the characters in the story. These are the 20 most famous portals in children's literature.

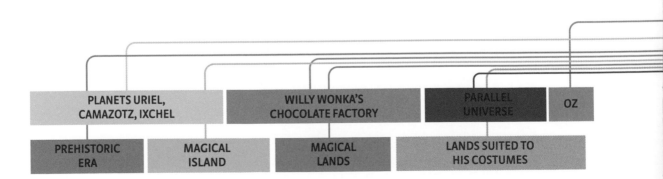

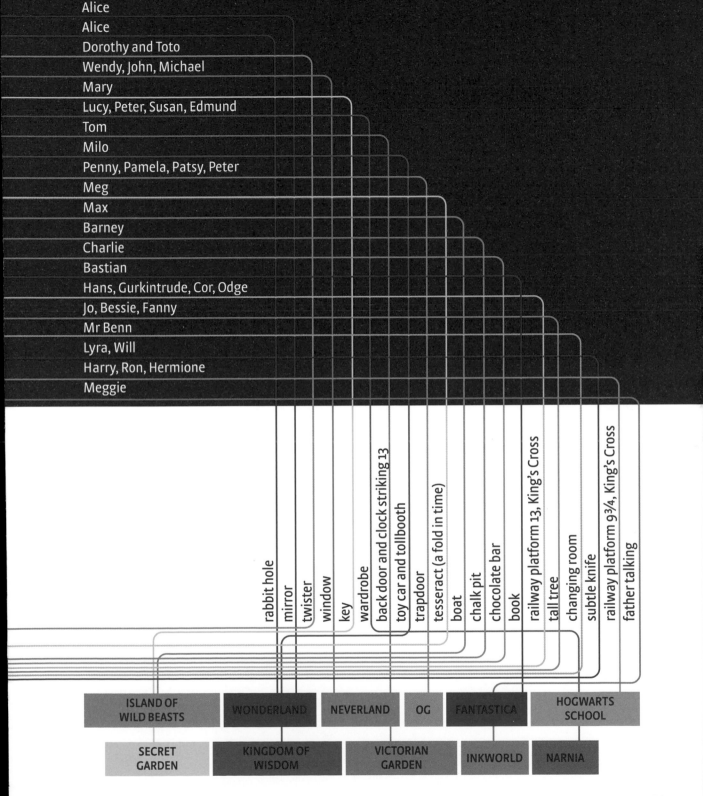

Alice
Alice
Dorothy and Toto
Wendy, John, Michael
Mary
Lucy, Peter, Susan, Edmund
Tom
Milo
Penny, Pamela, Patsy, Peter
Meg
Max
Barney
Charlie
Bastian
Hans, Gurkintrude, Cor, Odge
Jo, Bessie, Fanny
Mr Benn
Lyra, Will
Harry, Ron, Hermione
Meggie

rabbit hole
mirror
twister
window
key
wardrobe
back door and clock striking 13
toy car and tollbooth
trapdoor
tesseract (a fold in time)
boat
chalk pit
chocolate bar
book
railway platform 13, King's Cross
tall tree
changing room
subtle knife
railway platform 9¾, King's Cross
father talking

ISLAND OF WILD BEASTS
WONDERLAND
NEVERLAND
OG
FANTASTICA
HOGWARTS SCHOOL

SECRET GARDEN
KINGDOM OF WISDOM
VICTORIAN GARDEN
INKWORLD
NARNIA

DEGREES OF **GOTHIC**

Gothic literature has its beginnings in the late 18th century with Horace Walpole and Ann Radcliffe. They set a template that has been followed and improved upon by numerous writers ever since. Here are the 13 key ingredients of any true Gothic novel, and the great works of the genre gauged by how many each contains.

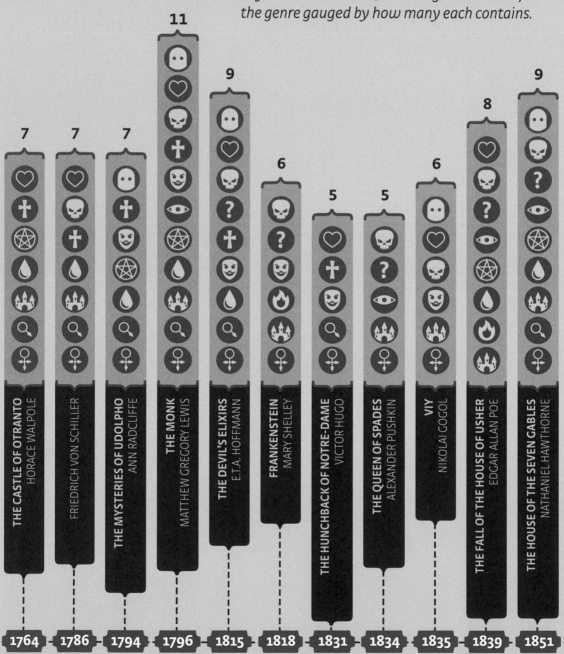

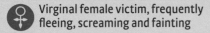

ESSENTIAL GOTHIC INGREDIENTS

- Virginal female victim, frequently fleeing, screaming and fainting
- Storms, fog or fire
- An ancestral curse or ancient prophecy
- Catholicism and clergy, monks and nuns
- Death, mourning, mortality
- Cruel, brooding male villain
- Bloodlines and aristocratic decay
- Visions, dreams and omens
- Madness
- Ghosts, witchcraft and devil worship, necromancy
- Crumbling, forbidding mansion or castle in a barren or remote landscape
- Sinister strangers, doppelgängers or monsters, deformity
- Lust, incest, rape, and suppressed dangerous female sexuality

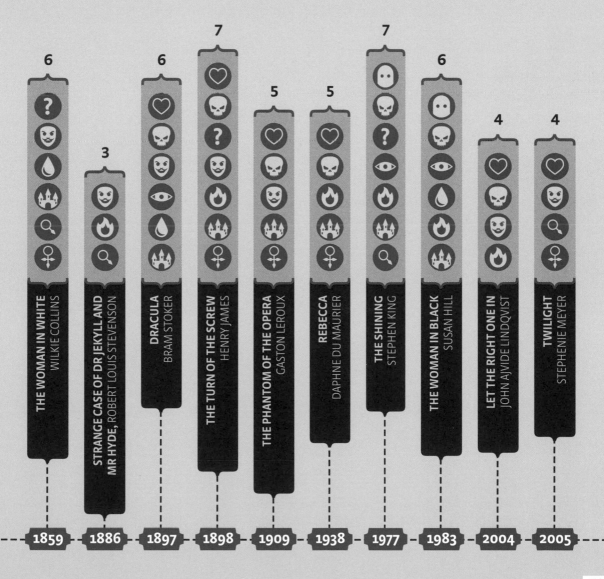

HERE BE **MONSTERS**

The Greeks knew how to create a good monster. Their fantastical creatures have stayed in the human psyche for centuries due partly to the retelling of original myths, and also because novelists and poets drew inspiration from them. Here are the most memorable interpretations of Greek monsters.

ENCELADUS
Giant with serpent-like limbs

HYPERION
John Keats
1819
Referenced

PIERRE
Herman Melville
1852
Appears in a dream

THE LOST HERO
Rick Riordan
2010
Primary villain

CENTAUR
Head and torso of a man, body of a horse

THE CHRONICLES OF NARNIA
C.S. Lewis
1950–1956
Creatures with reason

HARRY POTTER
J.K. Rowling
1997–2007
Centaurs live in the forbidden forest

THE CENTAUR
John Updike
1963
Reason and nature clash in a rural town

HARPIES
Bird women

HIS DARK MATERIALS
Philip Pullman
1995
Includes a race of winged women

THE LAST UNICORN
Peter S. Beagle
1968
The character Celeano embodies a harpy

A SONG OF ICE AND FIRE
George R.R. Martin
1996
Symbol of slaver families

BRIAREUS
1 of 3 giants with 100 hands and 50 heads

INFERNO
Dante
1308–1321
A giant in the 9th circle of hell

DON QUIXOTE
Miguel de Cervantes
1605
Believes windmills to be briareus

PARADISE LOST
John Milton
1667
Compared to fallen Satan

MANTICORE
Human head, sharp teeth, lion's body, scorpion's tail

THE MANTICORE
Robertson Davies
1972
Elements of subconscious manifest as manticore

HARRY POTTER
J.K. Rowling
1997–2007
Hagrid owns a manticore

MANY WATERS
Madeleine L'Engle
1986
Animal who eats other animals

MEDUSA
Gorgon, female monster with snakes for hair

THE LIGHTNING THIEF
Rick Riordan
2005
Main antagonist

A TALE OF TWO CITIES
Charles Dickens
1859
French aristocracy compared to Gorgons

MACBETH
William Shakespeare
1606
The three witches

ANTAEUS
A half-giant

INFERNO
Dante
1308–1321
Depicted as half-frozen giant

ANTAEUS (POEM)
Seamus Heaney
1975
Retelling

ANTAEUS (SHORT STORY)
Borden Deal
1962
Retelling

FAHRENHEIT 451
Ray Bradbury
1953
Metaphor for over-indulgence

LAMIA
Beautiful, evil queen

LAMIA
John Keats
1820
Tells of Hermes finding a lamia trapped in the body of a serpent

AURORA LEIGH
Elizabeth Barrett Browning
1856
Dead mother appears as lamia

ELEMENTALS: STORIES OF FIRE AND ICE
A.S. Byatt
1998
Lamia begins to be made human

NEVERWHERE
Neil Gaiman
1996
Lamia as warmth-drinking vampire

MINOTAUR
Head of a bull, body of a man

THE LION, THE WITCH AND THE WARDROBE
C.S. Lewis
1950
Followers of the Queen

THE HOUSE OF ASTERION
Jorge Borges
1947
Retelling the story of the minotaur

HOUSE OF LEAVES
Mark Z. Danielewski
2000
Minotaur and labyrinth central

STRANGE CASE OF DR JEKYLL AND MR HYDE
Robert Louis Stevenson
1886
Half man, half beast

PAN
Half man, half goat

ENDYMION
John Keats
1818
Festival of Pan

THE WIND IN THE WILLOWS
Kenneth Grahame
1908
Pan helps Rat and Mole

THE GREAT GOD PAN
Arthur Machen
1890
Symbol for power of nature

THE BLESSING OF PAN
Lord Dunsany
1927
Has a revival of worship of Pan

JITTERBUG PERFUME
Tom Robbins
1984
Pan appears throughout

IT'S THE END OF THE WORLD **(AGAIN)**

*The fashion for writing and reading dystopian novels of the
20th century peaked with Cold War hysteria, but showed signs
of a revival in interest just after the turn of this century.*

We *Yevgeny Zamyatin (1921)*

Brave New World *Aldous Huxley (1932)*

It Can't Happen Here *Sinclair Lewis (1935)*

Out Of The Silent Planet *C.S. Lewis (1938)*

Darkness At Noon *Arthur Koestler (1940)*

1984 *George Orwell (1948)*

The Day Of The Triffids *John Wyndham (1951)*

Fahrenheit 451 *Ray Bradbury (1953)*

The City And The Stars *Arthur C. Clarke (1956)*

Atlas Shrugged *Ayn Rand (1957)*

A Clockwork Orange *Anthony Burgess (1962)*

Logan's Run *William F. Nolan, George Clayton Johnson (1967)*

This Perfect Day *Ira Levin (1970)*

High Rise *J.G. Ballard (1975)*

Riddley Walker *Russell Hoban (1980)*

V For Vendetta *Alan Moore, David Lloyd (1988–89)*

Virtual Light *William Gibson (1993)*

Noughts And Crosses *Malorie Blackman (2001)*

Oryx And Crake *Margaret Atwood (2003)*

The Road *Cormac McCarthy (2006)*

The Hunger Games *Suzanne Collins (2008)*

Rondo *John Maher (2010)*

Station Eleven *Emily St. John Mandel (2014)*

UNESCO'S **MOST TRANSLATED**

The United Nations Organization for Education, Science and Culture compiled the top 30 authors by total of works each had in translation around the world, between 1979 and 2012. Here they are, with the number of each of the authors' original published works (short stories are collections) by genre.

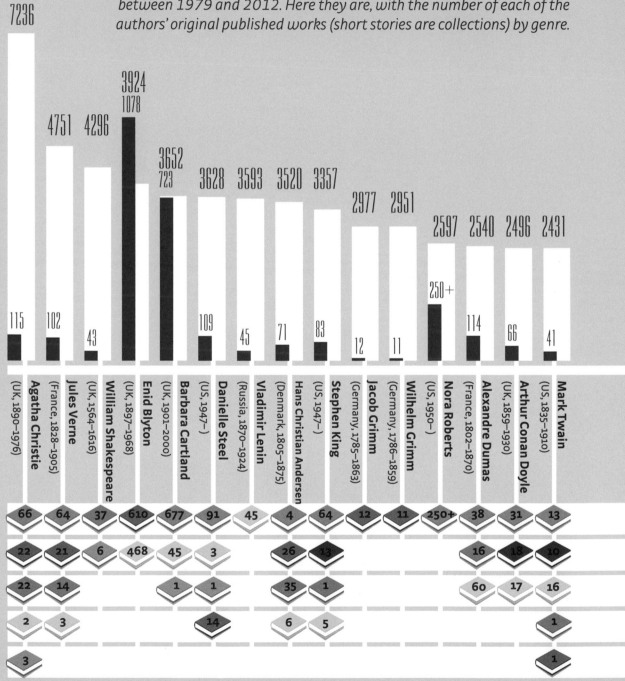

Author	Total	Genre breakdown
(UK, 1890–1976) **Agatha Christie**	7236 / 115	66, 22, 22, 2, 3
(France, 1828–1905) **Jules Verne**	4751 / 102	64, 21, 14, 3
(UK, 1564–1616) **William Shakespeare**	4296 / 43	37, 6
(UK, 1897–1968) **Enid Blyton**	3924 / 1078	610, 468
(UK, 1901–2000) **Barbara Cartland**	3652 / 723	677, 45, 1
(US, 1947–) **Danielle Steel**	3628 / 109	91, 3, 1, 14
(Russia, 1870–1924) **Vladimir Lenin**	3593 / 45	45
(Denmark, 1805–1875) **Hans Christian Andersen**	3520 / 71	4, 26, 35, 6
(US, 1947–) **Stephen King**	3357 / 83	64, 13, 1, 5
(Germany, 1785–1863) **Jacob Grimm**	2977 / 12	12
(Germany, 1786–1859) **Wilhelm Grimm**	2951 / 11	11
(US, 1950–) **Nora Roberts**	2597 / 250+	250+
(France, 1802–1870) **Alexandre Dumas**	2540 / 114	38, 16, 60
(UK, 1859–1930) **Arthur Conan Doyle**	2496 / 66	31, 18, 17, 1
(US, 1835–1910) **Mark Twain**	2431 / 41	13, 10, 16, 1, 1

TRANSLATIONS TOTAL
ORIGINAL TITLES

NOVEL · PLAY · POETRY · PHILOSOPHY · CHILDREN'S · COMIC BOOK · SHORT STORIES · NON-FICTION

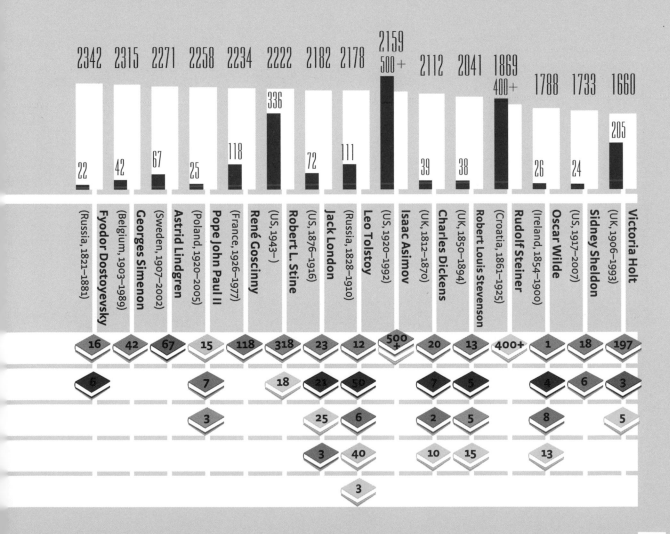

Author	Translations total	Original titles
Fyodor Dostoyevsky (Russia, 1821–1881)	2342	22
Georges Simenon (Belgium, 1903–1989)	2315	42
Astrid Lindgren (Sweden, 1907–2002)	2271	67
Pope John Paul II (Poland, 1920–2005)	2258	25
René Goscinny (France, 1926–1977)	2234	118
Robert L. Stine (US, 1943–)	2222	336
Jack London (US, 1876–1916)	2182	72
Leo Tolstoy (Russia, 1828–1910)	2178	111
Isaac Asimov (US, 1920–1992)	2159	500+
Charles Dickens (UK, 1812–1870)	2112	39
Robert Louis Stevenson (UK, 1850–1894)	2041	38
Rudolf Steiner (Croatia, 1861–1925)	1869	400+
Oscar Wilde (Ireland, 1854–1900)	1788	26
Sidney Sheldon (US, 1917–2007)	1733	24
Victoria Holt (UK, 1906–1993)	1660	205

LES MISÉRABLES
VICTOR HUGO
1862

0.18% *of work*   **823** *words*

SODOM AND GOMORRAH
VOLUME 4
of
In Search Of Lost Time
MARCEL PROUST
1913

0.45% *of work*   **944** *words*

ABSOLOM, ABSOLOM!
WILLIAM FAULKNER
1936

1.12% *of work*   **1,288** *words*

THE ROTTER'S CLUB
JONATHAN COE
2001

7.9% *of work*   **13,955** *words*

PERSONAL DAYS
ED PARKS
2008

18.8% *of work*   **16,000** *words*

DANCING LESSONS FOR THE ADVANCED IN AGE
BOHUMIL HRABAL
1964

100% *of work*   **20,000** *words*

THE LONGEST **SENTENCE**

Take a deep breath, and then begin reading. The longest sentence published in a single volume is currently 180,000 words long, and constitutes the whole of the book, in its original French language. Victor Hugo began the bizarre trend in the 19th century, since when these works have expanded on his idea of using the period sparingly.

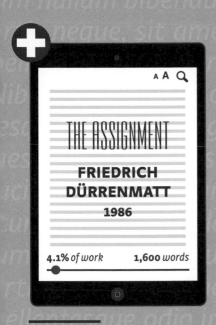

THE ASSIGNMENT

FRIEDRICH DÜRRENMATT

1986

4.1% *of work*   1,600 *words*

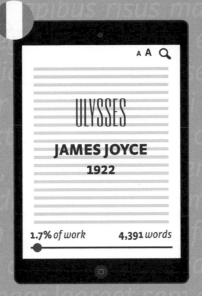

ULYSSES

JAMES JOYCE

1922

1.7% *of work*   4,391 *words*

AUTUMN OF THE PATRIARCH

GABRIEL GARCÍA MÁRQUEZ

1975

14.6% *of work*   13,650 *words*

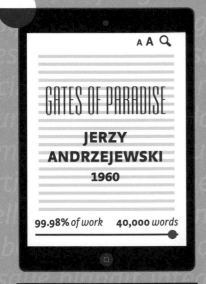

GATES OF PARADISE

JERZY ANDRZEJEWSKI

1960

99.98% *of work*   40,000 *words*

RAY OF THE STAR

LAIRD HUNT

2009

100% *of work*   58,000 *words*

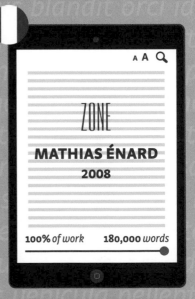

ZONE

MATHIAS ÉNARD

2008

100% *of work*   180,000 *words*

●————— = *percentage of work*

————— = *1,000 words*

Brother William of Baskerville
A Sherlock Holmes-style detective monk

Adso of Melk
William's much younger assistant (see Dr Watson)

THE LIBRARY/LABYRINTH

William and Adso use wool to find their way in and out of rooms looking for clues.

One room has hallucinogenic gas.

The centre of the library holds the secret to the Name Of The Rose.

AT THE MONASTERY

Abo of Fossanova – The abbot of the Benedictine monastery. Together with the librarian, his assistant and Jorge da Burgos, he is the only one who knows about the secrets of the library.

Jorge da Burgos – An old, blind former librarian of the monastery. A caricature of writer Jorge Luis Borges.

Severinus of Sankt Wendel – Herbalist who helps William.

Malachi of Hildesheim – Librarian.

Berengar of Arundel – Assistant librarian.

Adelmo of Otranto – Illuminator, novice. The first murder victim.

Venantius of Salvemec – Translator of manuscripts from Greek and Arabic and devoted to Aristotle.

Benno of Uppsala – Scandinavian student of rhetoric.

Ubertino   Michael   Bernardo   Bertrand

Rabano

Patrick

Alinardo of Grottaferrata – Eldest monk. Everyone believes he suffers from senile dementia but he will play a fundamental role in solving the mystery.

Remigio of Varagine – Cellarer. Name derived from Dominican friar Jacobus de Voragine, author of a Latin collection of the lives of the Saints.

Salvatore of Montferrat – Monk, associate of Remigio. Speaks a mixture of Latin and lewd vernacular Italian.

Nicholas of Morimondo – Glazier.

Aymaro of Alessandria – Italian transcriber. Gossipy and sneering.

Waldo of Hereford, Patrick of Clonmacnois, Rabano of Toledo – Transcribers.

OUTSIDERS

Ubertino of Casale – Franciscan friar in exile, friend of William.

Michael of Cesena – Leader of Spiritual Franciscans.

Bernardo Gui – Inquisitor from the Dominican order.

Bertrand del Poggetto – Cardinal and leader of the Papal legation.

Peasant girl from the village below the monastery – Adso has sex with her in the kitchen.

82

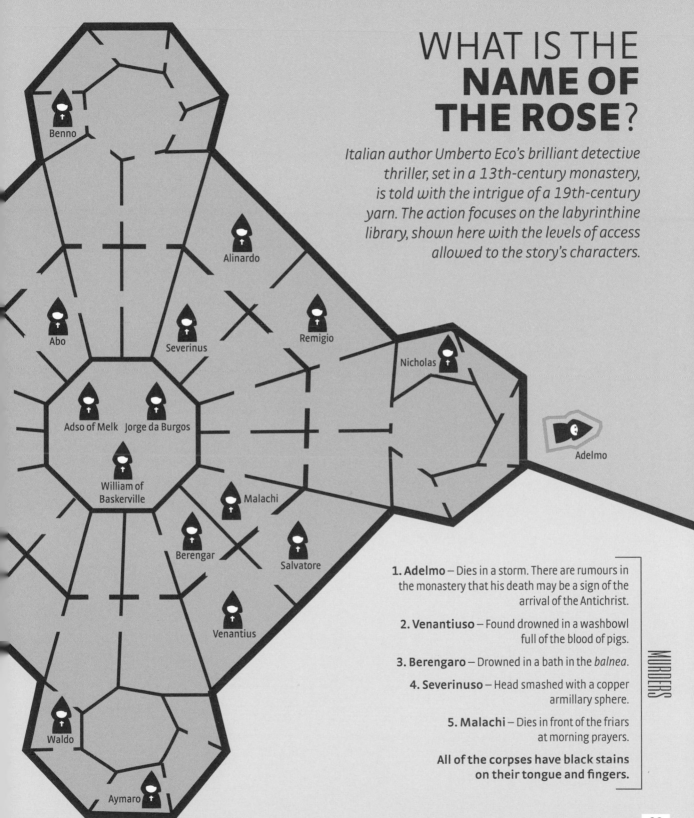

WHAT IS THE **NAME OF THE ROSE**?

Italian author Umberto Eco's brilliant detective thriller, set in a 13th-century monastery, is told with the intrigue of a 19th-century yarn. The action focuses on the labyrinthine library, shown here with the levels of access allowed to the story's characters.

Benno

Alinardo

Abo

Severinus

Remigio

Nicholas

Adso of Melk

Jorge da Burgos

William of Baskerville

Malachi

Berengar

Salvatore

Venantius

Waldo

Aymaro

Adelmo

MURDERS

1. **Adelmo** – Dies in a storm. There are rumours in the monastery that his death may be a sign of the arrival of the Antichrist.

2. **Venantiuso** – Found drowned in a washbowl full of the blood of pigs.

3. **Berengaro** – Drowned in a bath in the *balnea*.

4. **Severinuso** – Head smashed with a copper armillary sphere.

5. **Malachi** – Dies in front of the friars at morning prayers.

All of the corpses have black stains on their tongue and fingers.

JUDGING A BOOK **BY ITS COVER**

With the majority of books sold online rather than in-store, the tiny, cell phone-sized front cover image has to be able to convey content at a glance. Which is why the majority of genre-leading best-sellers tend to look the same, with only the author's name immediately recognizable. Here are the style rules for the eight best-selling genres.

GENRE

- Best-selling blockbuster mystery
- Classic literature
- Historical fiction
- Romantic suspense
- Erotica
- Vampire
- Chick-lit
- Teen horror

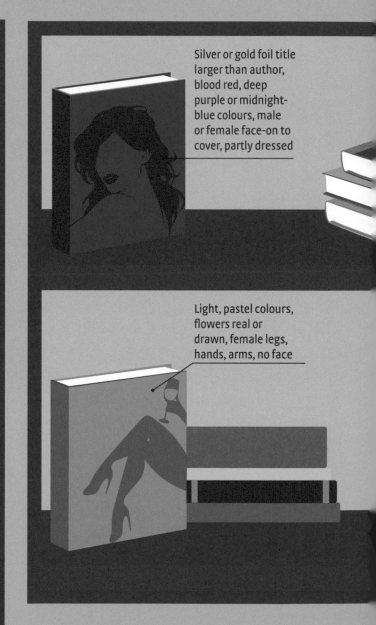

Silver or gold foil title larger than author, blood red, deep purple or midnight-blue colours, male or female face-on to cover, partly dressed

Light, pastel colours, flowers real or drawn, female legs, hands, arms, no face

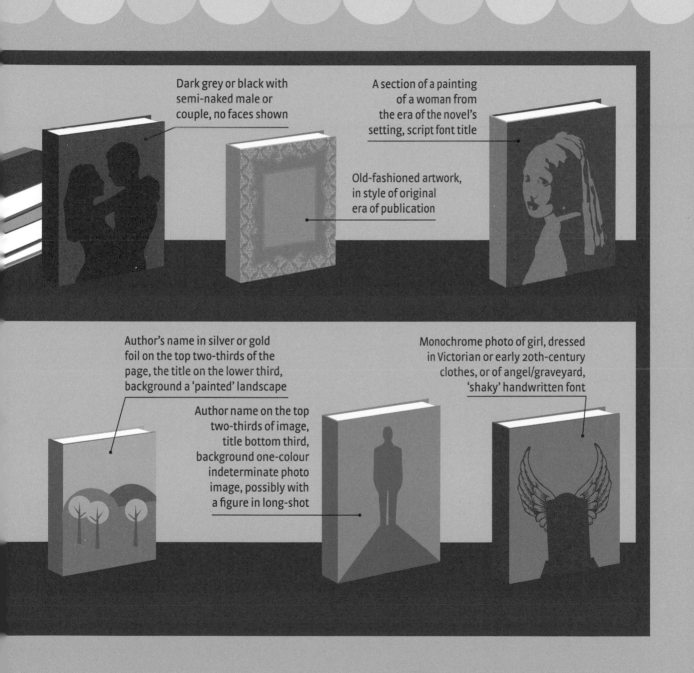

Dark grey or black with semi-naked male or couple, no faces shown

A section of a painting of a woman from the era of the novel's setting, script font title

Old-fashioned artwork, in style of original era of publication

Author's name in silver or gold foil on the top two-thirds of the page, the title on the lower third, background a 'painted' landscape

Author name on the top two-thirds of image, title bottom third, background one-colour indeterminate photo image, possibly with a figure in long-shot

Monochrome photo of girl, dressed in Victorian or early 20th-century clothes, or of angel/graveyard, 'shaky' handwritten font

DEATH BY **SHAKESPEARE**

William Shakespeare's tragedies are renowned for the number of deaths depicted (although often acted off-stage), and his history and 'problem' plays have a few characters meeting their maker, too. Here's how many and in which plays.

TITUS ANDRONICUS

Alarbus's arms and legs are cut off, then he is thrown into a fire

Chiron and Demetrius are stabbed then baked into a pie which Titus feeds to Tamora

Tamora is stabbed by Titus Andronicus

Lavinia's hands and tongue are cut off then she is stabbed

the Nurse is stabbed

Mutius is stabbed

Bassianus is stabbed

Martius and Quintus are beheaded

The Clown is hanged

Saturninus is stabbed

Titus is stabbed

...and Aaron is buried to his neck and starves

CORIOLANUS

Coriolanus is cut to pieces

TIMON OF ATHENS

Timon dies in the wilderness

THE WINTER'S TALE

Antigonus is eaten by a bear

...and Mamillius dies of grief

ROMEO & JULIET

Mercutio is stabbed

Tybalt is stabbed

Paris is stabbed

Romeo poisons himself

Juliet stabs herself

...and Lady Montague dies of grief

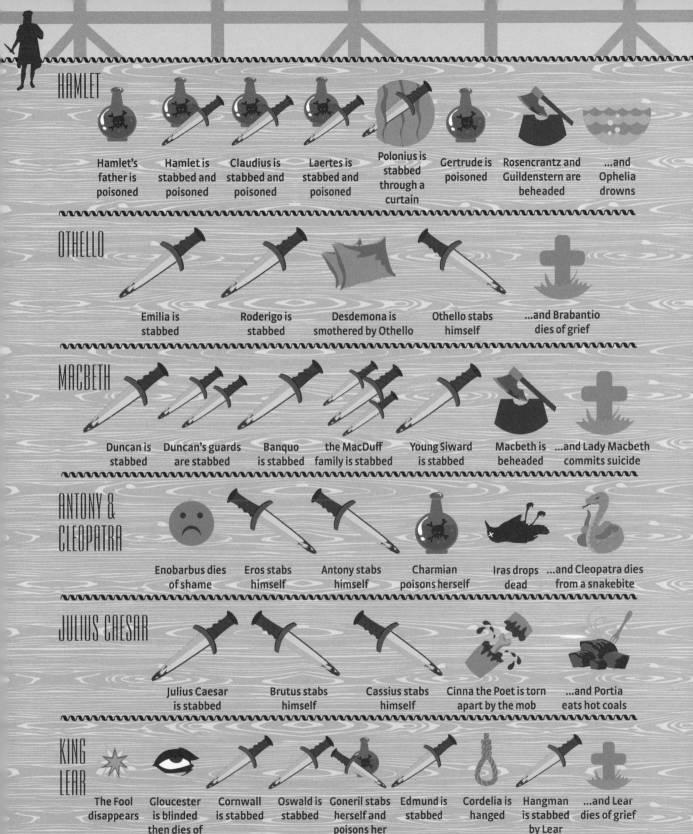

HAMLET

Hamlet's father is poisoned

Hamlet is stabbed and poisoned

Claudius is stabbed and poisoned

Laertes is stabbed and poisoned

Polonius is stabbed through a curtain

Gertrude is poisoned

Rosencrantz and Guildenstern are beheaded

...and Ophelia drowns

OTHELLO

Emilia is stabbed

Roderigo is stabbed

Desdemona is smothered by Othello

Othello stabs himself

...and Brabantio dies of grief

MACBETH

Duncan is stabbed

Duncan's guards are stabbed

Banquo is stabbed

the MacDuff family is stabbed

Young Siward is stabbed

Macbeth is beheaded

...and Lady Macbeth commits suicide

ANTONY & CLEOPATRA

Enobarbus dies of shame

Eros stabs himself

Antony stabs himself

Charmian poisons herself

Iras drops dead

...and Cleopatra dies from a snakebite

JULIUS CAESAR

Julius Caesar is stabbed

Brutus stabs himself

Cassius stabs himself

Cinna the Poet is torn apart by the mob

...and Portia eats hot coals

KING LEAR

The Fool disappears

Gloucester is blinded then dies of shock

Cornwall is stabbed

Oswald is stabbed

Goneril stabs herself and poisons her sister, Regan

Edmund is stabbed

Cordelia is hanged

Hangman is stabbed by Lear

...and Lear dies of grief

FROM STONE TABLET TO
DIGITAL TABLET

From scratches on a wall to scratches in the air, the history of man's published works has come a long way to nothing at all in the past 5,000 years.

C. 39,000BCE
The earliest European cave paintings made in a cave in El Castillo, Spain.

C. 3500BCE
Sumerian clay tablets with symbols pressed into clay using a triangular stylus.

2400BCE
First papyrus scrolls used in ancient Egypt.

1860
Beadle's Dime Novels are released in the US, printed on cheap, coarse paper, and sold for ten cents.

1832
Books published in illustrated paper jackets.

1934
Allen Lane adopts American paperback format in the UK to form Penguin Books.

1971
Michael Hart begins Project Gutenberg, the world's first online information provider, to make accessible literary works in the public domain.

1985
First CD-ROM format book; the American Encyclopedia.

200BCE
Wax tablet codex,
the beginning
of bound books used by
Greeks and Romans.

400–600CE
Illustrated, handwritten works in Europe
and the Middle East written on vellum-like
parchments made from calf, sheep,
or goat skins.

105CE
Paper invented by Cai Lun,
a Chinese eunuch, combining
'bark, hemp, old rags,
and used fish nets'.

1041
The Chinese invent movable
type; unsuccessful due
to the complexity
of Chinese alphabet.

1774
Chlorine is discovered,
later used to bleach
paper for print.

1501
Aldo Manuzio
designs and
produces the first
octavo book.

1440
Johannes Gutenberg completes
the first printing press, and
prints the 42-line Gutenberg
Bible in 1455.

1991
HTML code developed,
the internet made
available for commercial use.

1995
Jeff Bezos's Amazon.com
goes live, selling
books online.

1996
XML markup language
developed, streamlining
book production.

2011–2012
EPUB3 and HTML5
enable greater integration
of multimedia elements
within e-books.

2010
First Apple iPad
released
(plus iBooks
and iBooks Store).

2007
First Amazon
Kindle released,
as is EPUB
format.

2001–2006
E-books
developed for
the commercial
market.

GUESS THE **BEARDED** WRITER

From the 16th century to the present day, authors have grown their facial hair and trimmed it in interesting beard ways. Can you guess which facial hair belongs to whom? Clue: does not include George Eliot.

FRENCH
1580–90

FRENCH
1830–40

AMERICAN
1840–50

FRENCH
1850–60

RUSSIAN
1865–75

AMERICAN
1870–80

SWEDISH
1880–90

NATIONALITY

decade of key work

NORWEGIAN

1880–90

ENGLISH

1894–04

FRENCH

1910–20

AMERICAN

1925–35

GERMAN

1955–65

TRINIDADIAN

1960–70

CANADIAN

1970–80

NORWEGIAN

2000–10

TWO TRIBES: **THE MAHABHARATA**

The ancient Hindu text of the Mahabharata contains the eternal story of two warring tribal families who battle it out for supremacy and world domination. Each tribe member is either born with or attains a kind of super power.

PANDU
The father of the Pandavas, born pale, chose death over celibacy and founded a dynasty.

कौरव
Pandavas
The Good Guys (The Winners, with the Gods on their side)

KRISHNA
Incarnation of the God Vishnu: Wise, great tactician, advisor to the Pandavas and their protector. Imparts secret information on how to kill foes and ensures the Pandava victory.

KUNTI
Wife of Pandu also bore children for the Sun God, the Wind God, the God of Judgement, and the King of the Heavens. Raises her heroes sons single-handedly.

YUDHISTHIRA
Son of the God of Judgement. Rightful heir to the throne. Emperor of the World. Unblemished by sin or untruth.

BHIMA
Son of the Wind God. Strength of a thousand elephants. Bully. Killer of the 100 Kaurava brothers. Huge appetite.

DRAUPADI
Wife to the five brothers. Queen of unsurpassed beauty. Protected by Krishna. Highly virtuous, intelligent and compassionate.

ARJUNA
Lord of Heaven. Main hero, an unbeatable archer, peerless warrior and invincible in water bodies. Possesses divine weaponry. Single-handedly slayed 200,000 warriors to avenge the murder of his son.

NAKULA and SAHADEVA
Very handsome sons of the Twin Gods of Sunset and Sunrise. Nakula is a superior horse handler, swordsman and a master at Ayurveda. Sahadeva is a great astrologer with knowledge of the future, cursed with death if he reveals it.

BHISHMA

Grand-uncle of Dhritarashtra and Pandu and great man. Son of the Goddess of the Ganges. Vowed to serve. Chose time of his own death. Skilled in political science, attempted to minimize costs of the war.

SHAKUNI

Brother in law to Dhritarashtra, and resentful of him. Aims to destroy his clan. Possesses magic dice. Ruthless plotter, without honour.

पाण्डव
Kaurawas
The Bad Guys (Without the Gods on their side)

DHRITARASHTRA

Blind king. Bore a hundred sons. Ambitious, resentful of his brother's sons. Crusher of an iron statue.

DURYODHANA

Firstborn son. Hatred of Pandavas. Also Emperor of the World. Great military tactician. Acquires impenetrable body of diamond (except for lap). Symbolizes unfairness, deceit and lust.

GANDHARI

Wife to Dhritashtra. Self-imposed blindness. Bestows upon son impervious diamond-like body.

KARNA

Son of Sun God, firstborn of Kunti before marriage. Right hand to Duryodhana. Exemplary archer, possessed of divine weapon, denied opportunity because of low birth.

DUSHASANA

Second son. Obedient to older brother. Tried to disrobe Draupadi. Torn apart by Bhima, who drank his blood while Draupadi bathed her hair in it.

DRONACHARYA

Master archer, teacher of Arjuna. Bound by duty against love to fight with the Kauravas. Invincible warrior, slayed a vast amount of Pandava army. Committed suicide on being falsely informed of the death of his son.

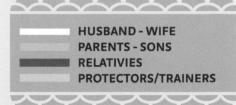

HUSBAND - WIFE
PARENTS - SONS
RELATIVIES
PROTECTORS/TRAINERS

$ 678M

$ 609M

$ 441M

Forrest Gump (1993)
Winston Groom (1986)

Life Of Pi (2013)
Yann Martel (2001)

The Exorcist (1973)
William Peter Blatty (1971)

$ 402M

$ 400M

$ 332M

Gone With the Wind (1939)
Margaret Mitchell (1936)

Dune (2021)
Frank Herbert (1965)

Schindler's List (1993)
Thomas Keneally (1982)

$ 236M

$ 188M

$ 186M

Silver Linings Playbook (2012)
Matthew Quick (2008)

12 Years a Slave (2013)
Solomon Northrup (1853)

The Horse Whisperer (1998)
Nicholas Evans (1995)

$ 34M

$ 27M

$ 38M

Carrie (1976)
Stephen King (1974)

A Clockwork Orange (1972)
Anthony Burgess (1962)

**James And The
Giant Peach** (1996)
Roald Dahl (1961)

$ 31M

$ 14M

$ 14M

**The Bridge On The
River Kwai** (1957)
Le Pont De La Rivière Kwai
Pierre Boulle (1952)

Vertigo (1958)
D'entre Les Morts
Pierre Boileau
and Pierre Ayraud (1954)

To Catch A Thief (1955)
David F. Dodge (1952)

SUCCESSFUL ADAPTATIONS

ADAPTATION

BOX OFFICE EARNINGS

Film Title (Year)
Book Title *if different
Author (Year)

Sometimes all a novel needs to become a best-seller is for a movie to be made of it. Smart authors write the screenplay of their novels – although not always – and re-publish the book of the film. Not that movie adaptations always work, and there have been many flop films of hit books.

UNSUCCESSFUL ADAPTATIONS

$ 17K

As I Lay Dying (2013)
William Faulkner (1930)

$ 120K

The Trial (1962)
Franz Kafka (1925)

$ 223K

Swann In Love (1984)
In Search of Lost Time
Marcel Proust (1913)

$ 1M

Don Quixote (1992)
Miguel de Cervantes
(1605–1615)

$ 2M

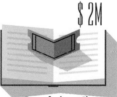

Crash (1996)
J.G. Ballard (1973)

$ 2M

American Pastoral (2016)
Philip Roth 1997

$ 2.3M

Ulysses (1967)
James Joyce (1922)

$ 3M

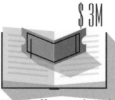

Mrs Dalloway (1997)
Virginia Woolf (1925)

$ 3M

Les Liaisons Dangereuses (1959)
Pierre Choderlos de Laclos (1782)

$ 3.7M

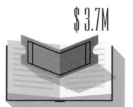

The Portrait of a Lady (1996)
Henry James (1881)

$ 4M

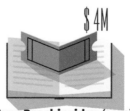

Myra Breckinridge (1970)
Gore Vidal (1969)

$ 5M

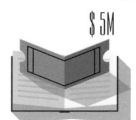

The Handmaid's Tale (1990)
Margaret Atwood (1985)

wikipedia.org, boxofficemojo.com

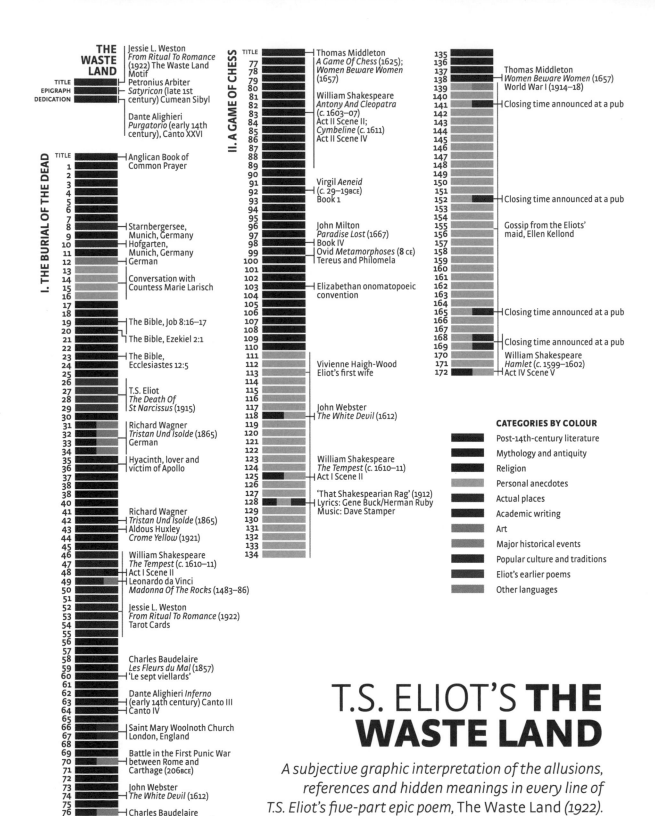

THE WASTE LAND

TITLE — Jessie L. Weston *From Ritual To Romance* (1922) The Waste Land Motif

EPIGRAPH — Petronius Arbiter *Satyricon* (late 1st century) Cumean Sibyl

DEDICATION — Dante Alighieri *Purgatorio* (early 14th century), Canto XXVI

I. THE BURIAL OF THE DEAD

TITLE — Anglican Book of Common Prayer
8–9 — Starnbergersee, Munich, Germany
10–11 — Hofgarten, Munich, Germany
12 — German
14–16 — Conversation with Countess Marie Larisch
19–20 — The Bible, Job 8:16–17
21 — The Bible, Ezekiel 2:1
23–24 — The Bible, Ecclesiastes 12:5
27–29 — T.S. Eliot *The Death Of St Narcissus* (1915)
31–33 — Richard Wagner *Tristan Und Isolde* (1865) German
35–36 — Hyacinth, lover and victim of Apollo
41–42 — Richard Wagner *Tristan Und Isolde* (1865)
43–44 — Aldous Huxley *Crome Yellow* (1921)
46–48 — William Shakespeare *The Tempest* (c. 1610–11) Act I Scene II
49–50 — Leonardo da Vinci *Madonna Of The Rocks* (1483–86)
52–54 — Jessie L. Weston *From Ritual To Romance* (1922) Tarot Cards
58–60 — Charles Baudelaire *Les Fleurs du Mal* (1857) 'Le sept viellards'
62–64 — Dante Alighieri *Inferno* (early 14th century) Canto III Canto IV
66–68 — Saint Mary Woolnoth Church London, England
69–71 — Battle in the First Punic War between Rome and Carthage (206BCE)
73–74 — John Webster *The White Devil* (1612)
76 — Charles Baudelaire *Les Fleurs du Mal* (1857) 'Au Lecteur', French

II. A GAME OF CHESS

TITLE
77–79 — Thomas Middleton *A Game Of Chess* (1625); *Women Beware Women* (1657)
81–86 — William Shakespeare *Antony And Cleopatra* (c. 1603–07) Act II Scene II; *Cymbeline* (c. 1611) Act II Scene IV
91–93 — Virgil *Aeneid* (c. 29–19BCE) Book 1
96–98 — John Milton *Paradise Lost* (1667) Book IV
99–100 — Ovid *Metamorphoses* (8 CE) Tereus and Philomela
103–104 — Elizabethan onomatopoeic convention
112–113 — Vivienne Haigh-Wood Eliot's first wife
117–118 — John Webster *The White Devil* (1612)
123–125 — William Shakespeare *The Tempest* (c. 1610–11) Act I Scene II
127–129 — 'That Shakespearian Rag' (1912) Lyrics: Gene Buck/Herman Ruby Music: Dave Stamper

135–138 — Thomas Middleton *Women Beware Women* (1657)
139 — World War I (1914–18)
141 — Closing time announced at a pub
152 — Closing time announced at a pub
155–156 — Gossip from the Eliots' maid, Ellen Kellond
165 — Closing time announced at a pub
168–169 — Closing time announced at a pub
170–172 — William Shakespeare *Hamlet* (c. 1599–1602) Act IV Scene V

CATEGORIES BY COLOUR

- Post-14th-century literature
- Mythology and antiquity
- Religion
- Personal anecdotes
- Actual places
- Academic writing
- Art
- Major historical events
- Popular culture and traditions
- Eliot's earlier poems
- Other languages

T.S. ELIOT'S **THE WASTE LAND**

A subjective graphic interpretation of the allusions, references and hidden meanings in every line of T.S. Eliot's five-part epic poem, The Waste Land *(1922).*

Line	Reference
TITLE	Buddha, The Fire Sermon
173	
174	Edmund Spenser
175	*Prothalamion* (1596)
176	The River Thames
177	
178	
179	
180	The Bible, Psalm 137;
181	Lake Geneva, where Eliot
182	worked on *The Waste Land*
183	while on rest-cure
184	
185	Andrew Marvell
186	*To His Coy Mistress* (c. 1650s)
187	
188	
189	
190	William Shakespeare
191	*The Tempest* (c. 1610–11)
192	Act I Scene II
193	
194	
195	John Day
196	*The Parliament Of Bees*
197	(c. 1608–16);
198	Diana and Actaeon
199	Ballad of unknown origin
200	Reported to Eliot in
201	Sydney, Australia
202	Paul Verlaine, *Parsifal* (1888);
203	Richard Wagner, *Parsifal* (1877);
204	Holy Grail, French
205	Tereus and Philomela
206	Charles Baudelaire
207	*Les Fleurs Du Mal* (1857)
208	'Le sept viellards'
209	Smyrna, Turkey, focus of the
210	Greco-Turkish War (1919–22)
211	Trading abbreviation from
212	Eliot's time at Lloyds Bank
213	Cannon Street Hotel,
214	London, England
215	Metropole Hotel,
216	Brighton, England
217	
218	
219	
220	
221	Sappho Fragment 149 (7BCE)
222	
223	Tiresias
224	
225	
226	
227	
228	
229	
230	
231	
232	
233	
234	Manufacturing town
235	of Bradford, England
236	
237	
238	
239	
240	
241	Sophocles
242	*Antigone*
243	(c. 442BCE);
244	*Oedipus Rex*
245	(c. 429BCE);
246	Homer *Odyssey*
247	(late 8th century BCE)
248	
249	
250	
251	Oliver Goldsmith
252	*The Vicar Of*
253	*Wakefield* (1762)
254	
255	William Shakespeare
256	*The Tempest* (c. 1610–11)
257	Act I Scene II
258	
259	Streets running parallel to
260	the River Thames, London

Line	Reference
261	
262	
263	Ionic columns in the
264	Church of St Magnus
265	the Martyr, London,
266	England
267	
268	
269	
270	
271	
272	
273	
274	
275	The River Thames at
276	Greenwich, London, England
277	Richard Wagner, *Die*
278	*Götterdämmerung* (1874)
279	James Anthony Froude
280	*History Of England From The*
281	*Fall Of Wolsey To The Death*
282	*Of Elizabeth* (1850–70)
283	
284	
285	
286	
287	
288	
289	
290	
291	Dante Alighieri
292	*Purgatorio* (early
293	14th century), Canto V
294	Richmond and Kew,
295	London, England
296	Moorgate, London,
297	England
298	
299	Margate, where Eliot
300	worked on *The Waste*
301	*Land* while on rest-cure
302	
303	
304	
305	
306	St Augustine *Confessions*
307	(397–398CE)
308	Buddha, The Fire Sermon
309	
310	
311	

Line	Reference
TITLE	
312	
313	
314	
315	T.S. Eliot
316	*Dans Le Restaurant* (1920)
317	
318	
319	
320	
321	

Line	Reference
TITLE	
322	
323	
324	
325	
326	
327	
328	
329	
330	
331	
332	
333	The Bible, Matthew 26–27
334	
335	
336	
337	
338	
339	
340	
341	
342	
343	
344	

Line	Reference
345	The Bible, Matthew 26–27
346	
347	
348	
349	
350	
351	
352	
353	
354	
355	
356	Sound of the hermit-thrush that
357	Eliot heard in Quebec County
358	
359	
360	
361	Sir Ernest Shackleton,
362	*South* (1919);
363	The Bible, Luke 24
364	
365	
366	
367	
368	
369	
370	Hermann Hesse
371	*Blick Ins Chaos* (1922);
372	Post-World War I Europe
373	
374	Jerusalem, Athens, Alexandria
375	Vienna, London
376	Charles Baudelaire
377	*Les Fleurs du Mal* (1857)
378	'Le sept viellards'
379	
380	
381	
382	
383	
384	
385	Jessie L. Weston *From Ritual*
386	*To Romance* (1922)
387	The Perilous Chapel
388	
389	
390	
391	French onomatopoeic
392	convention
393	
394	
395	The Ganges River, India
396	
397	The Himalayas, Sanskrit
398	
399	
400	
401	Sanskrit
402	
403	Dante Alighieri *Inferno*
404	(early 14th century) Canto V
405	
406	
407	John Webster
408	*The White Devil* (1612)
409	
410	
411	Dante Alighieri *Inferno*
412	(early 14th century)
413	Canto XXXIII; F.H. Bradley
414	*Appearance And Reality* (1893)
415	
416	William Shakespeare
417	*Coriolanus* (c. 1605–08)
418	Coriolanus, Roman war hero
419	
420	
421	Jessie L. Weston
422	*From Ritual To Romance* (1922)
423	The Fisher King
424	The Bible, Isaiah 38:1
425	Nursery rhyme, 'London Bridge'
426	Dante Alighieri *Purgatorio* (early
427	14th century) Canto XXVI, Italian
428	*Peruigilium Veneris*, Latin;
429	Tereus and Philomela
430	Gerard de Nerval *El Desdichado*
431	(1854), French
432	Thomas Kyd *The Spanish*
433	*Tragedie* (1592)
	Brihadaranyaka Upanishad

Brihadaranyaka Upanishad, The Three Disciples

SHAKEN, STIRRED AND SOZZLED

Vodka martini, 'shaken not stirred' – often said as part of a bad Sean Connery impersonation – is one of the most quotable lines from Bond. Yet Her Majesty's top secret agent's love of the bottle would leave him impotent and at death's door.

Bond would be classified in the **'higher risk'** of problem drinkers and would be at **high risk of liver damage, an early death and impotence**.

Daily units of alcohol

13	● **Bond's** average daily drinking habit
12	
11	
10	
9	● **Higher risk** (regular) drinkers
8	
7	
6	
5	● **Increasing risk** (regular) drinkers
4	
3	● **Lower risk** (irregular) drinkers
2	
1	

Doctors analyzing the Ian Fleming novels show James Bond polishes off the equivalent of **one and a half bottles of wine every day**.

They say he is **not the man to trust to deactivate a nuclear bomb**.

Books on shelf (left to right):

CASINO ROYALE 1953
LIVE AND LET DIE 1954
MOONRAKER 1955
DIAMONDS ARE FOREVER 1956
FROM RUSSIA, WITH LOVE 1957
DR NO 1958
GOLDFINGER 1959

Doctors in Derby and Nottingham sat down to read the **14 BOND NOVELS** in their spare time. With a notebook at hand they charted every day and every drink.

FOR YOUR EYES ONLY 1960
THUNDERBALL 1961
THE SPY WHO LOVED ME 1962
ON HER MAJESTY'S SECRET SERVICE 1963
YOU ONLY LIVE TWICE 1964
THE MAN WITH THE GOLDEN GUN 1965
OCTOPUSSY AND THE LIVING DAYLIGHTS 1966

Total **alcohol consumed** throughout the 14 novels:

IN 88 DAYS	1 WEEK	1 DAY	36 DAYS
1,150 UNITS OF ALCOHOL	**92** UNITS OF ALCOHOL	**5** VODKA MARTINIS	**SOBER** IN HOSPITAL, PRISON, REHAB

 = 10 units

This is **four times the recommended maximum intake** for men in the UK.

MOBY-DICK
BY NUMBERS

Moby-Dick; or, The Whale (1851) by former merchant seaman-turned-author Herman Melville was out of print when he died in 1891, aged 72, and his obituary in The New York Times misspelled the title. Yet it is now regarded as one of the greatest works of American fiction to have been written. It's a book as big as the white whale was described as being.

WHALE SIZE

Ishmael's calculations of the size of the largest sperm whale:
85–90ft long, 40ft circumference, weight 90 tons; 20 ribs, each from 6ft to 8ft long.

21st-century adult sperm whales:
measures between 49–59ft (15–18m) and weighs between 35–45 tons.

The story of Moby-Dick was inspired by the sinking of the 87ft (27m) whaling ship Essex in 1820 by a whale that survivors claimed was 85ft (26m) long.

Average price sperm whale meat and oil (1850):
$300 (£150) per whale

Price of ambergris:
1 gold guinea per ounce

THE BOOK

Number of words total: **209,117**

Number of chapters total: **135**

Shortest chapter: #122 (Midnight, Aloft), **36 words**

Longest chapter: #54 (The Town-Ho's Story), **7,938 words**

Number of chapters before casting off to sea: **21**

Number of chapters before Ahab appears: **27**

Number of chapters before Moby-Dick is sighted: **132**

THE STORY

Narrator and sole survivor of the voyage – **Ishmael**

Whaling ship for the voyage – **The *Pequod***

Captain of the *Pequod* – **Ahab** (58 years old)

Number of characters named after biblical characters
(Ishmael from Genesis, Ahab and Elijah both from Books of Kings)

Number of crew members on the *Pequod*

Number of nationalities in the crew

Number of other whaling ships met during the voyage

Number of other whaling ships to sight Moby-Dick

Number of harpooners on the *Pequod*

Number of American harpooners on the *Pequod* (Tashtego)

Number of whales killed by the *Pequod* before meeting Moby-Dick

Number of multinational coffee chains named after a character in
the book (Starbucks)

Number of whalers killed by Moby-Dick during
the voyage not on the *Pequod*

Number of *Pequod* crew killed by Moby-Dick

Number of sea captains killed by Moby-Dick on the voyage

Number of limbs consumed by Moby-Dick

Number of limbs made out of whale bone

Number of garments made out of whale penis

HOW AN IDEA BECOMES **A BOOK**

In an effort to demystify the publishing business, here's how an idea can take one of five different routes to publication. Whether a first-time author, a best-selling writer, celebrity, hip website owner or a publisher originating the process in-house, these are the steps the process can take from the beginning to end.

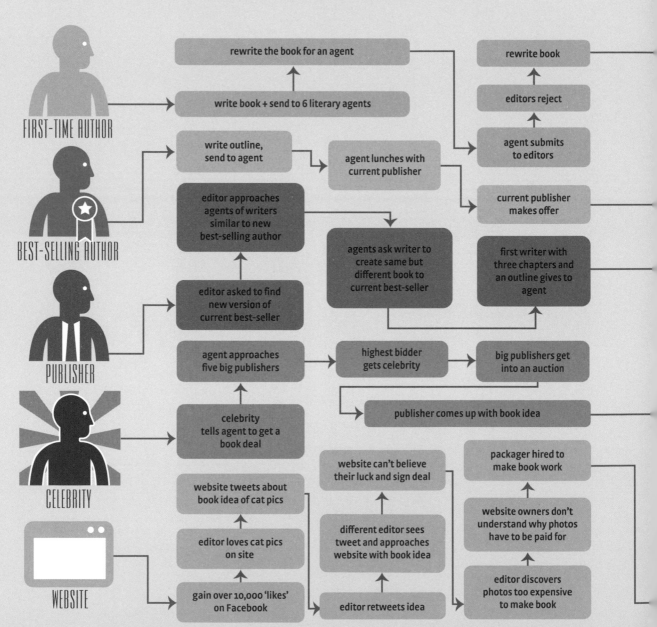

FIRST-TIME AUTHOR

rewrite the book for an agent

write book + send to 6 literary agents

rewrite book

editors reject

agent submits to editors

BEST-SELLING AUTHOR

write outline, send to agent

agent lunches with current publisher

current publisher makes offer

editor approaches agents of writers similar to new best-selling author

agents ask writer to create same but different book to current best-seller

first writer with three chapters and an outline gives to agent

PUBLISHER

editor asked to find new version of current best-seller

agent approaches five big publishers

highest bidder gets celebrity

big publishers get into an auction

CELEBRITY

celebrity tells agent to get a book deal

publisher comes up with book idea

packager hired to make book work

website can't believe their luck and sign deal

WEBSITE

website tweets about book idea of cat pics

editor loves cat pics on site

different editor sees tweet and approaches website with book idea

website owners don't understand why photos have to be paid for

gain over 10,000 'likes' on Facebook

editor retweets idea

editor discovers photos too expensive to make book

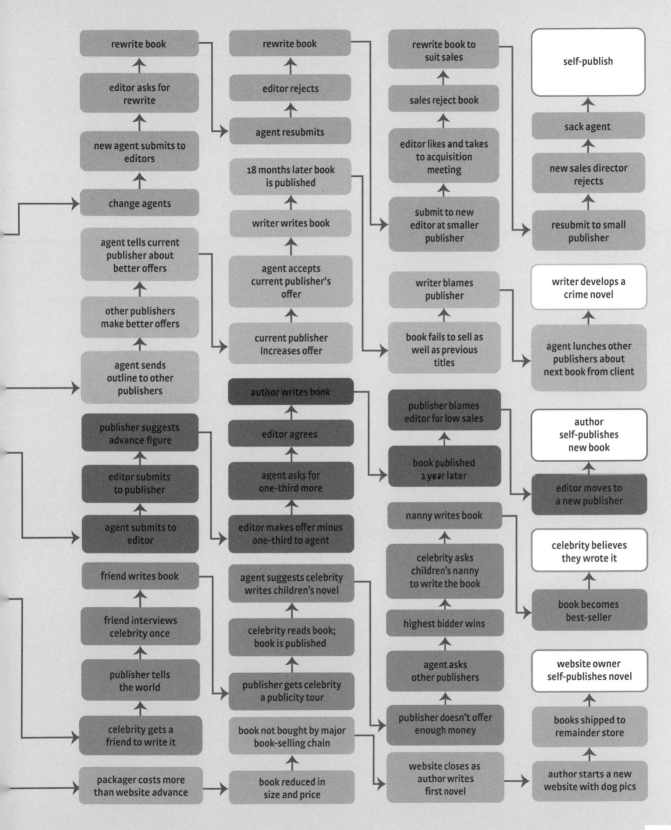

rewrite book ← editor asks for rewrite ← new agent submits to editors ← change agents

agent tells current publisher about better offers ← other publishers make better offers ← agent sends outline to other publishers

publisher suggests advance figure ← editor submits to publisher ← agent submits to editor

friend writes book ← friend interviews celebrity once ← publisher tells the world ← celebrity gets a friend to write it

packager costs more than website advance

rewrite book ← editor rejects ← agent resubmits

18 months later book is published ← writer writes book ← agent accepts current publisher's offer ← current publisher Increases offer

author writes book ← editor agrees ← agent asks for one-third more ← editor makes offer minus one-third to agent

agent suggests celebrity writes children's novel ← celebrity reads book; book is published ← publisher gets celebrity a publicity tour ← book not bought by major book-selling chain ← book reduced in size and price

rewrite book to suit sales ← sales reject book ← editor likes and takes to acquisition meeting ← submit to new editor at smaller publisher

writer blames publisher ← book fails to sell as well as previous titles

publisher blames editor for low sales ← book published 1 year later

nanny writes book ← celebrity asks children's nanny to write the book ← highest bidder wins ← agent asks other publishers ← publisher doesn't offer enough money ← website closes as author writes first novel

self-publish ← sack agent ← new sales director rejects ← resubmit to small publisher

writer develops a crime novel ← agent lunches other publishers about next book from client

author self-publishes new book ← editor moves to a new publisher

celebrity believes they wrote it ← book becomes best-seller

website owner self-publishes novel ← books shipped to remainder store ← author starts a new website with dog pics

103

CITY LITS

When choosing a setting for a work of fiction, the choice of city can determine what kind of story the author is embarking upon. Some cities have so many disparate styles of story set in them that they have an anomalous meaning, but these six have become representative of a particular style of fiction.

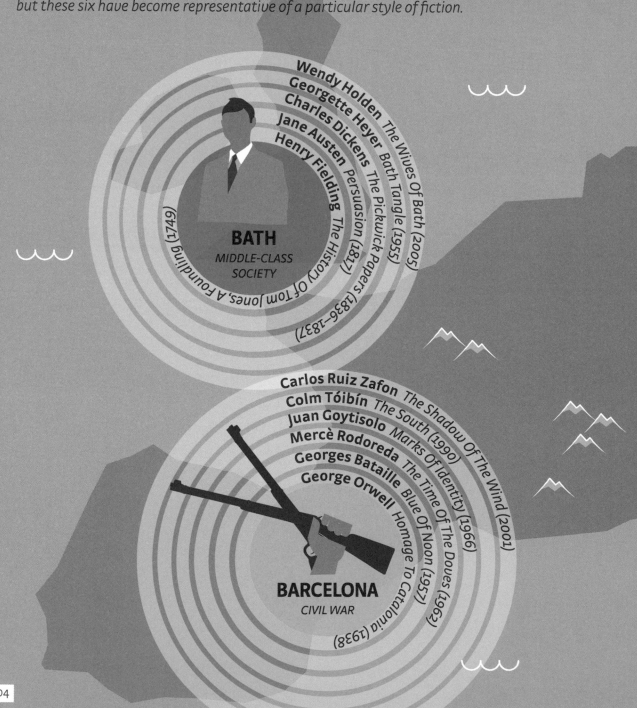

Wendy Holden *The Wives Of Bath* (2005)
Georgette Heyer *Bath Tangle* (1955)
Charles Dickens *The Pickwick Papers* (1836–1837)
Jane Austen *Persuasion* (1817)
Henry Fielding *The History Of Tom Jones, A Foundling* (1749)

BATH
MIDDLE-CLASS SOCIETY

Carlos Ruiz Zafon *The Shadow Of The Wind* (2001)
Colm Tóibín *The South* (1990)
Juan Goytisolo *Marks Of Identity* (1966)
Mercè Rodoreda *The Time Of The Doves* (1957)
Georges Bataille *Blue Of Noon* (1962)
George Orwell *Homage To Catalonia* (1938)

BARCELONA
CIVIL WAR

BERLIN
DECADENCE

Sven Regener Herr Lehmann/Berlin Blues (2001)
Wladimir Kaminer Russian Disco (2000)
Philip Kerr March Violets (1989)
Christiane F. Wir Kinder von Bahnhof Zoo (1979)
Christopher Isherwood Goodbye To Berlin (1939)
Alfred Döblin Berlin Alexanderplatz (1929)

ST PETERSBURG
TURMOIL

Helen Dunmore The Siege (2001)
J.M. Coetzee The Master Of St Petersburg (1994)
Victor Serge The Conquered City (1975)
Leo Tolstoy War And Peace (1869)
Fyodor Dostoyevsky Crime And Punishment (1866)
Alexander Pushkin The Captain's Daughter (1835)

PRAGUE
LOST IDENTITY

Jachym Topol City Sister Silver (1994)
Milan Kundera The Unbearable Lightness Of Being (1984)
Vladimir Nabokov Despair (1934)
Hermann Ungar The Maimed (1923)
Gustav Meyrink The Golem (1914)

VENICE
GOOD & EVIL

Sally Vickers Miss Garnet's Angel (2000)
Ian McEwan The Comfort Of Strangers (1981)
Daphne du Maurier Don't Look Now (1971)
Thomas Mann Death In Venice (1912)
Henry James The Wings Of A Dove (1902)
Wilkie Collins The Haunted Hotel (1879)

105

LITERARY CUTS

Guess the female author from her hairstyle.

ENGLISH
1800–1815

ENGLISH
1818–1830

ENGLISH
1840–1850

FRENCH
1830–1860

FRENCH
1900–1945

ENGLISH
1915–1940

DANISH
1926–1956

NATIONALITY

Prime period

FRENCH

AMERICAN

ENGLISH

1940–1970

1970–1980

AMERICAN

AMERICAN

1992–2013

GERMAN-ROMANIAN

1950–1990

1980–2000

ENGLISH

ENGLISH

1997–2007

1980–2000

2011–2013

THE **GROWLERY**

Dogs have always been much more useful to people than cats; as a hunting aid, a source of heat and energy, and a guard against attack. It's little wonder that stories involving canine characters stretch back to the pre-Greek era. In this handy dog matrix, the four aspects of doggy behaviour attest to the versatility of the species as a literary device.

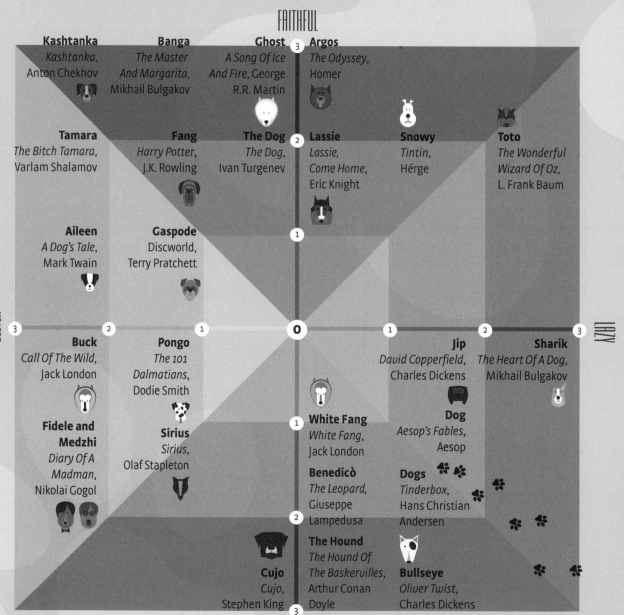

FAITHFUL

Kashtanka
Kashtanka,
Anton Chekhov

Banga
*The Master
And Margarita*,
Mikhail Bulgakov

Ghost
*A Song Of Ice
And Fire*, George
R.R. Martin

3

Argos
The Odyssey,
Homer

Tamara
The Bitch Tamara,
Varlam Shalamov

Fang
Harry Potter,
J.K. Rowling

The Dog
The Dog,
Ivan Turgenev

2

Lassie
*Lassie,
Come Home*,
Eric Knight

Snowy
Tintin,
Hérge

Toto
*The Wonderful
Wizard Of Oz*,
L. Frank Baum

Aileen
A Dog's Tale,
Mark Twain

Gaspode
Discworld,
Terry Pratchett

1

CLEVER 3 — 2 — 1 — **0** — 1 — 2 — 3 **LAZY**

Buck
Call Of The Wild,
Jack London

Pongo
*The 101
Dalmatians*,
Dodie Smith

Jip
David Copperfield,
Charles Dickens

Sharik
The Heart Of A Dog,
Mikhail Bulgakov

1

White Fang
White Fang,
Jack London

Dog
Aesop's Fables,
Aesop

**Fidele and
Medzhi**
*Diary Of A
Madman*,
Nikolai Gogol

Sirius
Sirius,
Olaf Stapleton

Benedicò
The Leopard,
Giuseppe
Lampedusa

Dogs
Tinderbox,
Hans Christian
Andersen

2

The Hound
*The Hound Of
The Baskervilles*,
Arthur Conan
Doyle

Cujo
Cujo,
Stephen King

Bullseye
Oliver Twist,
Charles Dickens

3

EVIL

108

AGE SHALL NOT WITHER THEM

While poets have been published at an early age (Neruda was 14, Rimbaud 15, Walcott 18), the average age of debut novelists is in their 30s. Which makes these youngest and oldest debut novelists truly exceptional.

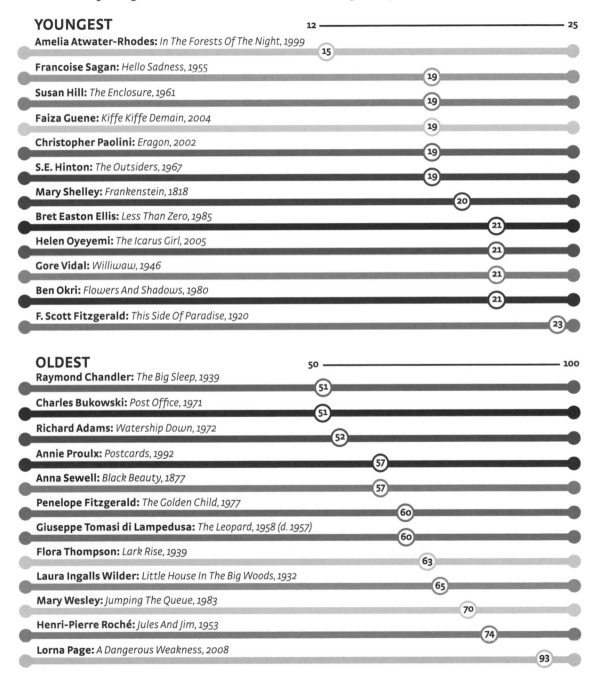

YOUNGEST

12 — 25

Amelia Atwater-Rhodes: *In The Forests Of The Night, 1999* — 15

Francoise Sagan: *Hello Sadness, 1955* — 19

Susan Hill: *The Enclosure, 1961* — 19

Faiza Guene: *Kiffe Kiffe Demain, 2004* — 19

Christopher Paolini: *Eragon, 2002* — 19

S.E. Hinton: *The Outsiders, 1967* — 19

Mary Shelley: *Frankenstein, 1818* — 20

Bret Easton Ellis: *Less Than Zero, 1985* — 21

Helen Oyeyemi: *The Icarus Girl, 2005* — 21

Gore Vidal: *Williwaw, 1946* — 21

Ben Okri: *Flowers And Shadows, 1980* — 21

F. Scott Fitzgerald: *This Side Of Paradise, 1920* — 23

OLDEST

50 — 100

Raymond Chandler: *The Big Sleep, 1939* — 51

Charles Bukowski: *Post Office, 1971* — 51

Richard Adams: *Watership Down, 1972* — 52

Annie Proulx: *Postcards, 1992* — 57

Anna Sewell: *Black Beauty, 1877* — 57

Penelope Fitzgerald: *The Golden Child, 1977* — 60

Giuseppe Tomasi di Lampedusa: *The Leopard, 1958 (d. 1957)* — 60

Flora Thompson: *Lark Rise, 1939* — 63

Laura Ingalls Wilder: *Little House In The Big Woods, 1932* — 65

Mary Wesley: *Jumping The Queue, 1983* — 70

Henri-Pierre Roché: *Jules And Jim, 1953* — 74

Lorna Page: *A Dangerous Weakness, 2008* — 93

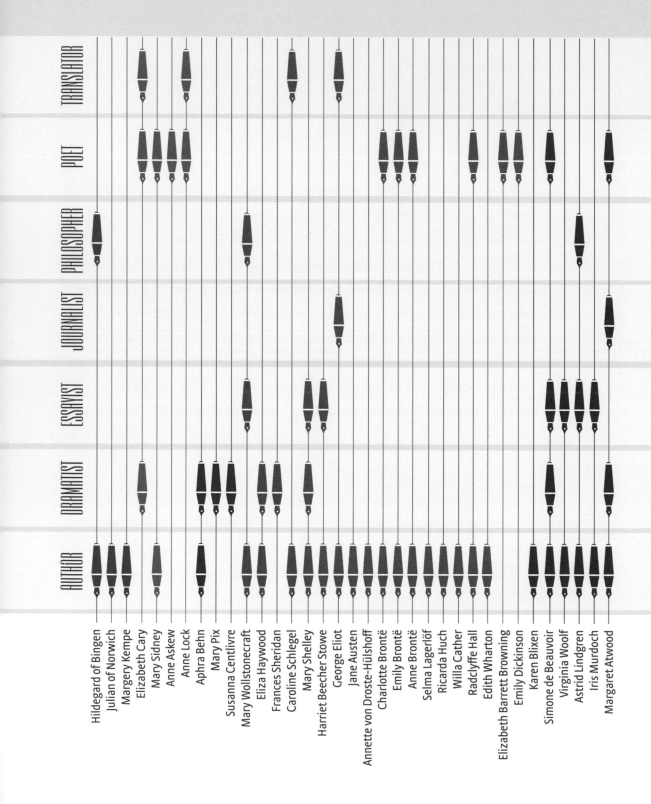

A ROOM OF **ONE'S OWN**

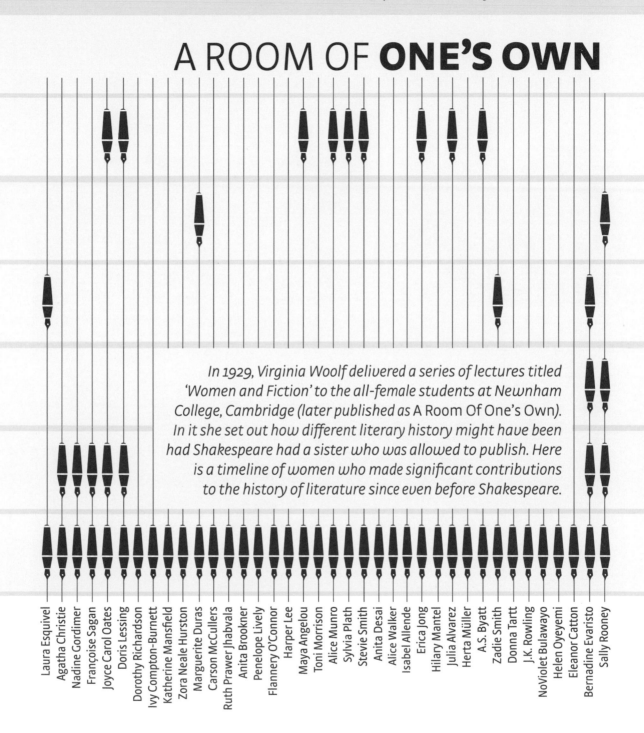

In 1929, Virginia Woolf delivered a series of lectures titled 'Women and Fiction' to the all-female students at Newnham College, Cambridge (later published as A Room Of One's Own). In it she set out how different literary history might have been had Shakespeare had a sister who was allowed to publish. Here is a timeline of women who made significant contributions to the history of literature since even before Shakespeare.

Laura Esquivel · Agatha Christie · Nadine Gordimer · Françoise Sagan · Joyce Carol Oates · Doris Lessing · Dorothy Richardson · Ivy Compton-Burnett · Katherine Mansfield · Zora Neale Hurston · Marguerite Duras · Carson McCullers · Ruth Prawer Jhabvala · Anita Brookner · Penelope Lively · Flannery O'Connor · Harper Lee · Maya Angelou · Toni Morrison · Alice Munro · Sylvia Plath · Stevie Smith · Anita Desai · Alice Walker · Isabel Allende · Erica Jong · Hilary Mantel · Julia Alvarez · Herta Müller · A.S. Byatt · Zadie Smith · Donna Tartt · J.K. Rowling · NoViolet Bulawayo · Helen Oyeyemi · Eleanor Catton · Bernadine Evaristo · Sally Rooney

DULCE ET **DECORUM EST**

There were soldier authors who fought, wrote and died in the trenches of World War I. Among them were novelists, playwrights and poets, some of whom perished not in battle, but years later. They will always be remembered for the work they wrote about the experiences of war, whatever side of no man's land they stood.

Wilfred Owen
BRITAIN
ARMY, 2ND LIEUTENANT, MILITARY CROSS
18 Mar. 1893 † 4 Nov. 1918
Died in Sambre-Oise Canal, France
Cause: killed in action

Rupert Brooke
BRITAIN
NAVY, SUB-LIEUTENANT
3 Aug. 1887
† 23 Apr. 1917
Died in hospital ship off Skypos, Greece
Cause: sepsis from mosquito bite

Ivor Gurney
BRITAIN
ARMY, SOLDIER
28 Feb. 1890 † 26 Dec. 1937
Died in London, England
Cause: tuberculosis

Robert Graves
BRITAIN
ARMY, SOLDIER
27 Jul. 1895 † 7 Dec. 1985
Died in Majorca, Spain
Cause: heart failure

Gilbert Frankau
BRITAIN
ARMY, STAFF CAPTAIN
21 Apr. 1884 † 4 Nov. 1952
Died in London, England
Cause: lung cancer

John Roderigo dos Passos
UNITED STATES
AMBULANCE CORPS
14 Jan. 1896 † 28 Sept. 1970
Died in Baltimore, MD
Cause: heart failure

Edward Cummings
UNITED STATES
AMBULANCE CORPS
14 Oct. 1894 † 3 Sept. 1962
Died in Conway, NH
Cause: stroke

George Bernanos
FRANCE
ARMY, SOLDIER
20 Feb. 1888 † 5 Jul. 1948
Died in Neuilly sur Seine, France
Cause: cancer

PO Poet   **PL** Playwright   **N** Novelist

PO

Edward Thomas
BRITAIN
ARMY, 2ND LIEUTENANT
3 Mar. 1878
† 9 Apr. 1917
Died in Pas de Calais, France
Cause: sniper fire

PO

John McCrae
CANADA
ARMY, FIELD SURGEON
30 Nov. 1872 † 28 Jan. 1918
Died in Boulogne sur Mer, France
Cause: pneumonia

PO **N**

Robert W. Service
CANADA
AMBULANCE CORPS
16 Jan. 1874
† 11 Sept. 1958
Died in Lancieux, France
Cause: natural causes

N **PL**

Ilya Grigoryevich Ehrenburg
RUSSIA
WAR CORRESPONDENT
27 Jan. 1891 † 31 Aug. 1967
Died in Moscow, Russia
Cause: prostate cancer

PO **PL**

August Stramm
GERMANY
ARMY, COMMANDER, IRON CROSS
29 Jul. 1874 † 1 Sept. 1915
Died in Horodec Kobryn, Belarus
Cause: killed in action

N **PO** **PL**

Franz Werfel
GERMANY
ARMY, PROPAGANDIST
10 Sept. 1890
† 25 Aug. 1945
Died in New York, NY
Cause: heart failure

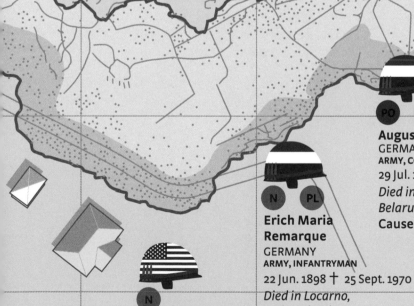
N **PL**

Erich Maria Remarque
GERMANY
ARMY, INFANTRYMAN
22 Jun. 1898 † 25 Sept. 1970
Died in Locarno, Switzerland
Cause: aneurysm

N

Ernest Hemingway
UNITED STATES
AMBULANCE CORPS
21 Jul. 1899 † 2 Jul. 1961
Died in Ketchum, ID
Cause: suicide

N

Ernst Jünger
GERMANY
ARMY, LIEUTENANT
29 Mar. 1895 † 17 Feb. 1998
Died in Riedlingen, Germany
Cause: natural causes

NOSTALGIA
IS WHAT IT
USED TO BE

The Color Purple
Alice Walker

Roots
Alex Haley

Gone With The Wind
Margaret Mitchell

Treasure Island
Robert Louis Stevenson

War And Peace
Leo Tolstoy

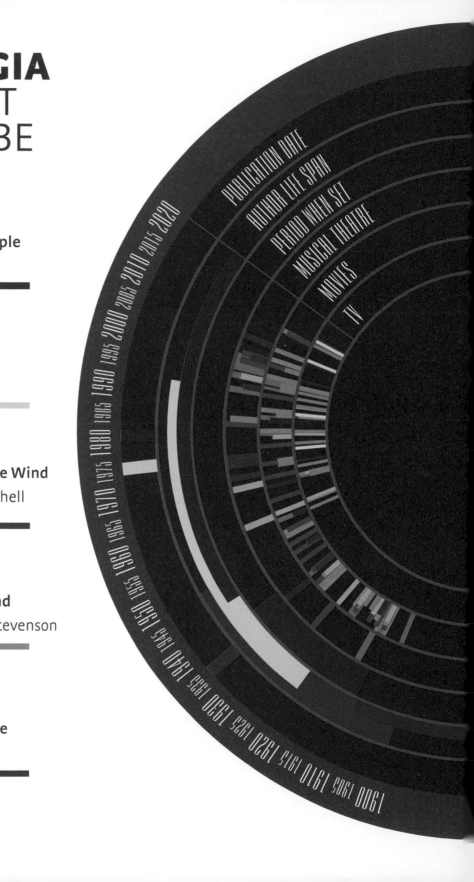

PUBLICATION DATE
AUTHOR LIFE SPAN
PERIOD WHEN SET
MUSICAL THEATRE
MOVIES
TV

2020 2015 2010 2005 2000 1995 1990 1985 1980 1975 1970 1965 1960 1955 1950 1945 1940 1935 1930 1925 1920 1915 1910 1905 1900

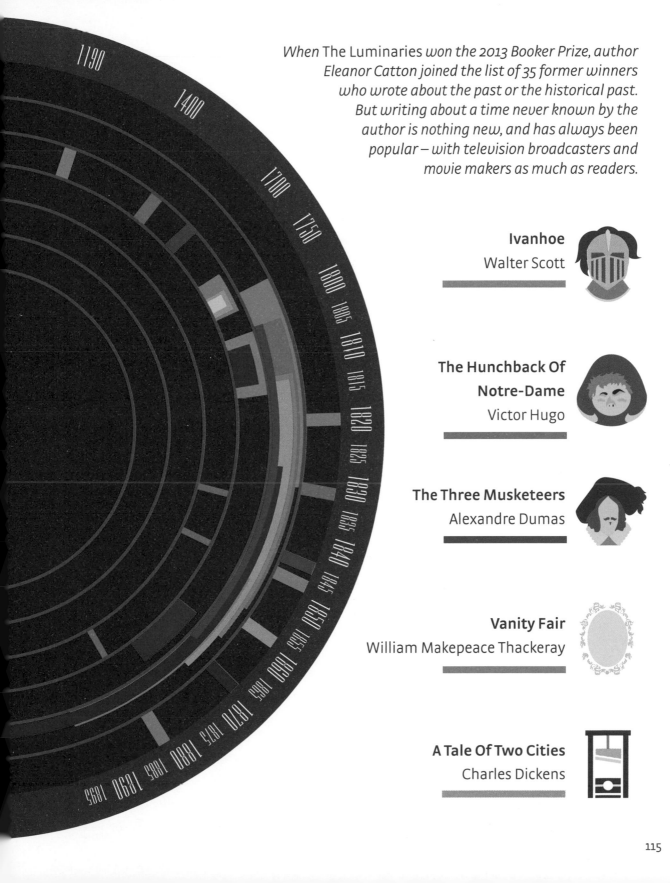

When The Luminaries *won the 2013 Booker Prize, author Eleanor Catton joined the list of 35 former winners who wrote about the past or the historical past. But writing about a time never known by the author is nothing new, and has always been popular – with television broadcasters and movie makers as much as readers.*

Ivanhoe
Walter Scott

The Hunchback Of Notre-Dame
Victor Hugo

The Three Musketeers
Alexandre Dumas

Vanity Fair
William Makepeace Thackeray

A Tale Of Two Cities
Charles Dickens

1190 1400 1700 1750 1800 1805 1810 1815 1820 1825 1830 1835 1840 1845 1850 1855 1860 1865 1870 1875 1880 1885 1890 1895

DEATH IN DISCWORLD

The character of Death has appeared in all but two of the 41 books written by Terry Pratchett in the Discworld series between 1983 and his tragic passing (mourned by millions) in 2015. There are five titles in which Death is the central character. As with all Pratchett's work, they are filled with allusions and references beyond the obvious. Here's what each one is really about.

Number of allusions referenced ?

Mort
1987

12, 1, 11, 7, 7

Reaper Man
1991

12, 4, 7, 6, 6, 3, 2, 11

Soul Music
1994

2, 10, 15, 15, 35, 56, 5, 1

Hogfather
1996

17, 9, 8, 5, 11, 1, 38, 6

Thief Of Time
2001

8, 4, 2, 5, 1, 1, 7

Totals

47, 27, 41, 68, 20, 4, 102, 42

film

classic literature

myth, folklore

previous Pratchett works

music

television

politicians

miscellaneous

ON THE **SONNET***

The most popular sonnet form was first used by a now little-read Italian poet named Jacopo da Lentini, circa 1210–1260. After his 14-line format was adopted by countrymen Dante Alighieri and Petrarch in the following century, the sonnet as we know it became a staple of poetry. Here, in 14 poets and one of their key works laid out in rhyme schemes, is a history of the sonnet from 1266 to 2013.

POET (DATES)	KEY SONNET (DATE)	NATIONALITY
Dante Alighieri 1266–1321	*A Casan'alma Presa e Gentil Core* 1295	ITALIAN
Petrarch 1304–1874	*Una Candida Cerva* 1368	ITALIAN
Thomas Wyatt 1503–1542	*Whoso List To Hunt* 1536–1540	ENGLISH
William Shakespeare 1564–1616	*Sonnet #18, Shall I Compare Thee To A Summer's Day?* 1609	ENGLISH
John Donne 1572–1631	*Holy Sonnet #10, Death Be Not Proud* 1633	ENGLISH
John Milton 1608–1674	*When I Consider How My Light Is Spent* 1652	ENGLISH
William Wordsworth 1770–1850	*The World Is Too Much With Us* 1802–1804	ENGLISH
Percy Bysshe Shelley 1792–1822	*Ozymandias* 1817	ENGLISH
Charles Baudelaire 1821–1867	*Autumn Sonnet* 1857	FRENCH
Dante Gabriel Rossetti 1828–1882	*A Sonnet (From The House Of Life)* 1870	ENGLISH
Rainer Maria Rilke 1875–1926	*Die Sonneten An Orpheus #29* 1922	GERMAN
Edna St Vincent Millay 1892–1950	*I, Being Born A Woman And Distressed* 1923	AMERICAN
Pablo Neruda 1904–1973	*100 Love Sonnets #17* 1959	ARGENTINIAN
Seamus Heaney 1939–2013	*A Dream Of Jealousy* 1979	IRISH

RHYME SCHEME

A ▲ B ♥ C ● D ◗ E ■ F ✚ G ♠ H ◆ I ▮ J ✔ K ✦ L (M ❖ N ✖

BOOKS FOR COOKS

Not all books with recipes in them have been written by celebrity chefs. Some have been penned by the greatest novelists and playwrights in the world, as this menu of dishes taken from numerous titles proves.

MENU 1397 – 1977

SOUPS

- Borscht — 1933
- Clam chowder with pounded ship's biscuits — 1851
- Soupe à la tortue à la Louisianne *(Turtle soup)* — 1958

STARTERS

- Omelette with biscuits — 1869
- Avocado pear stuffed with crabmeat and mayonnaise — 1963
- Pickled herring *(Twelfth Night)* — 1602
- Crayfish — 1933
- Partridge wing *(Much Ado About Nothing)* — 1599
- Cold chicken slices — 1963
- Salted pork flakes in butter — 1851
- Spiced beef jellies — 1913
- Hot venison pasty *(The Merry Wives Of Windsor)* — 1602

MAIN DISHES

PORK
- Gammon of bacon *(Henry IV Part 1)* — 1597
- Bacon and ham — 1820

BEEF
- Corned beef and potatoes — 1869
- Beef and mustard *(The Taming Of The Shrew)* — 1592
- Beef with stewed plums — 1933
- Rare roast beef — 1963

LAMB
- Joint of mutton *(Henry IV Part 2)* — 1599

CHICKEN & GAME
- Chicken en casserole — 1933
- Pigeon pie — 1820
- Quails in coffins — *1958*
- Duck with onion sauce — 1820
- Roasted crane — c.1387

FISH & SEAFOOD
- Fish poached in white wine, capers and sorrels — 1977

MONDAY

- Blankmanger — c.1387
  (rice boiled in almond milk, with chunks of chicken or fish)

TUESDAY

- Blinis Demidof a l'Oobleck — 1958

WEDNESDAY

- Jakke of Dover — c.1387
  (stale meat or fish pie/pasty, dressed in blood or gravy to make it appear fresh)

THURSDAY

- Broil'd tripe — 1592
  (The Taming Of The Shrew)

FRIDAY

- Whale steak — 1851

HOUSE SPECIALTIES

A DOZEN OYSTERS
1933

BLACK CAVIAR
1963

LOBSTER
1869

SIDES

- Bread rubbed with garlic — 1933
- Sop *(toasted bread or cake dipped in wine)* — c.1387
- Wastel-breed *(fine white bread)* — c.1387
- Garleek, oynons and lekes — c.1387
- Asparagus (with butter) — 1869/1913
- New potatoes — 1913/1933
- Mustard gratin — 1977
- Stewed tripe — 1977

DESSERTS

- Stewed prunes — 1602
  (The Merry Wives Of Windsor)
- Buttered slapjacks (pancakes) with honey — 1820
- Blancmange and strawberries — 1869
- Madeleines — 1913
- Cherry tartlets shaped like boats — 1913
- Chocolate cake — 1913
- Sweet pudding — 1933
- Roquefort cheese — 1933
- Marzipan fruit — 1963

MENU KEY

- *The Canterbury Tales* Geoffrey Chaucer (1387–1400)
- *The Complete Works Of Shakespeare* William Shakespeare (c.1590–1613)
- *The Legend Of Sleepy Hollow* Washington Irving (1820)
- *Moby-Dick* Herman Melville (1851)
- *Little Women* Louisa May Alcott (1868–69)
- *In Search Of Lost Time* Marcel Proust (1913)
- *Down And Out In Paris And London* George Orwell (1933)
- *Babette's Feast* Isak Dinesen (1958)
- *The Bell Jar* Sylvia Plath (1963)
- *The Flounder* Günter Grass (1977)

BEVERAGES

BEERS

- Bragot *(drink of fermented ale, honey and spices)* — c.1387
- A jubbe of London ale — c.1387

WINES

- Vernage *(sweet Italian wine)* — c.1387
- Wyn — c.1387
- Ypocras *(spiced wine)* — c.1387

THANKS, BUT **NO THANKS**

To be awarded a major prize for anything is usually considered to be a crowning achievement. However, there have been 15 authors who refused major prizes for their work (or refused nominations); here's who they were, and why they said 'thanks, but no thanks'.

1906
Leo Tolstoy (Russian)
Nobel Prize
$100,000
Refused on the grounds that the prize money 'may only bring evil.'

1926
Sinclair Lewis (American)
Pulitzer Prize
$10,000
Rejected the jury as an authority to judge literature.

1964
Jean-Paul Sartre (French)
Nobel Prize
$100,000
Refused, stating that 'A writer should not allow himself to be turned into an institution.'

1988
Ursula K. Le Guin (American)
Nebula Prize
Objected to the Science Fiction Writers of America's refusing a Polish novelist honorary membership.

1925
George Bernard Shaw (Irish)
Nobel Prize
$100,000
Took the prize because his wife convinced him to, but refused the money.

1958
Boris Pasternak (Russian)
Nobel Prize
$100,000
His government disapproved of the Western award.

1970
Aleksandr Solzhenitsyn (Russian)
Nobel Prize
$100,000
Would not leave Russia to receive the prize.

2003

**Hari Kunzru
(English)**

John Llewellyn Rhys Prize

$8,400 (£5,000)

Objected to the xenophobic views of prize's sponsor, the *Mail on Sunday*.

2011

**Michael Ondaatje
(Sri Lankan-Canadian)**

Scotiabank Giller Prize

Thought that he had received it too many times already, and should not enter again.

2012

**Javier Marías
(Spanish)**

Spanish National Narrative Prize

$27,400 (€20,000)

Prize is state-funded and he is against receiving public money.

2006

**Peter Handke
(Austrian)**

Heinrich Heine German Literature Prize

$68,500 (€50,000)

Accepted then rejected the prize after German politicians opposed his perceived support of Slobodan Milosevic.

2008

**Adolf Muschg
(German)**

Swiss Book Prize

$68,500 (€50,000)

Compared the prize to a TV reality show spectacle and said he didn't write for that kind of reception.

2011

**Alice Oswald
(English),
John Kinsella
(Australian)**

Poetry Book Society T.S. Eliot Prize

$25,000 (£15,000)

Declined nomination because of a sponsorship deal with an investment company.

2012

**Lawrence Ferlinghetti
(American)**

Pannonius Prize

$68,500 (€50,000)

Because the award is funded in part by the repressive Hungarian government.

2014

**Allan Ahlberg
(British)**

Booktrust Lifetime Achievement Award

Objected to the award being sponsored by Amazon, on account of their non-payment of taxes.

Upper West Side

Time-travelling advertising artist meets a promiscuous college teacher

Simon Morley of Jack Finney's *Time And Again* meets **Theresa Dunn** of Judith Rossner's *Looking For Mr Goodbar*

Harlem

Con man using black politics meets invisible man born of black politics

Deke O'Hara of Chester Himes's *Cotton Comes To Harlem* meets the **unnamed narrator** of Ralph Ellison's *Invisible Man*

Central Park

Teenage rebel meets self-absorbed flapper

Holden Caulfield of J.D. Salinger's *Catcher In The Rye* meets **Daisy Buchanan** of F. Scott Fitzgerald's *The Great Gatsby*

Greenwich Village

Suicidal jazz drummer meets depressed journalist

Rufus Scott of James Baldwin's *Another Country* meets **Esther Greenwood** of Sylvia Plath's *The Bell Jar*

Washington Square

Shy, plain, reluctant heiress with overbearing father meets reluctant heir with overbearing father

Catherine Sloper of Henry James's *Washington Square* meets **Mike Corleone** of Mario Puzo's *The Godfather*

Wall Street

Stock Exchange terrorist meets self-styled Master Of The Universe

Lyle of Don DeLillo's *Players* meets **Sherman McCoy** of Tom Wolfe's *Bonfire Of The Vanities*

Lower Manhattan

Lonely rich businessman meets lonely rich music label owner

George Smith of J.P. Donleavy's *A Singular Man* meets **Bennie Salazar** from Jennifer Egan's *A Visit From The Goon Squad*

Lower Broadway

Architect supremacist meets reluctant sleuth

Howard Roark of Ayn Rand's *The Fountainhead* meets **Nick Charles** of Dashiell Hammett's *The Thin Man*

Fifth Avenue

Fantasizing society girl meets fantasizing countess

Holly Golightly of Truman Capote's *Breakfast At Tiffany's* meets **Countess Ellen Olenska** of Edith Wharton's *The Age Of Innocence*

Lexington

Murderous amoral investment banker meets avenging amoral vigilante

Patrick Bateman of Bret Easton Ellis's *American Psycho* meets **Rorschach** of *Watchmen*

Empire State Building

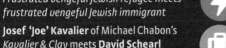

Frustrated vengeful Jewish refugee meets frustrated vengeful Jewish immigrant

Josef 'Joe' Kavalier of Michael Chabon's *Kavalier & Clay* meets **David Schearl** of Henry Roth's *Call It Sleep*

Williamsburg

Orthodox Jewish teenage math genius meets book-loving Jewish teen

Reuven Malter of Chaim Potok's *The Chosen* meets **Francie Nolan** of Betty Smith's *A Tree Grows In Brooklyn*

Midtown

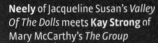

Egotistical actress meets abused Macy's assistant

Neely of Jacqueline Susan's *Valley Of The Dolls* meets **Kay Strong** of Mary McCarthy's *The Group*

Brooklyn

Private investigator with Tourette's Syndrome meets transvestite prostitute

Essrog of Jonathan Lethem's *Motherless Brooklyn* meets **Georgette** of Hubert Selby Jr's *Last Exit To Brooklyn*

East Broadway

Nine-year-old with a dead dad meets lonely old man with imaginary friend

Oskar Schell of Jonathan Safran Foer's *Extremely Loud And Incredibly Close* meets **Leo Gursky** of Nicole Krauss's *The History Of Love*

Brooklyn Heights

Fictional fiction author meets concentration camp survivor

Daniel Quinn of Paul Auster's *New York Trilogy* meets **Sophie Zawistowska** of William Styron's *Sophie's Choice*

Lower East Side

Morally challenged bar manager meets morally challenged copy-editor

Eric Cash of Richard Price's *Lush Life* meets **Asa Leventhal** of Saul Bellow's *The Victim*

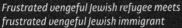

MEET ME IN
NEW YORK

Imagining the literary characters of different centuries and authors meeting at the great locations of New York where their stories are set.

IN MEMORIAM
A.H.H.

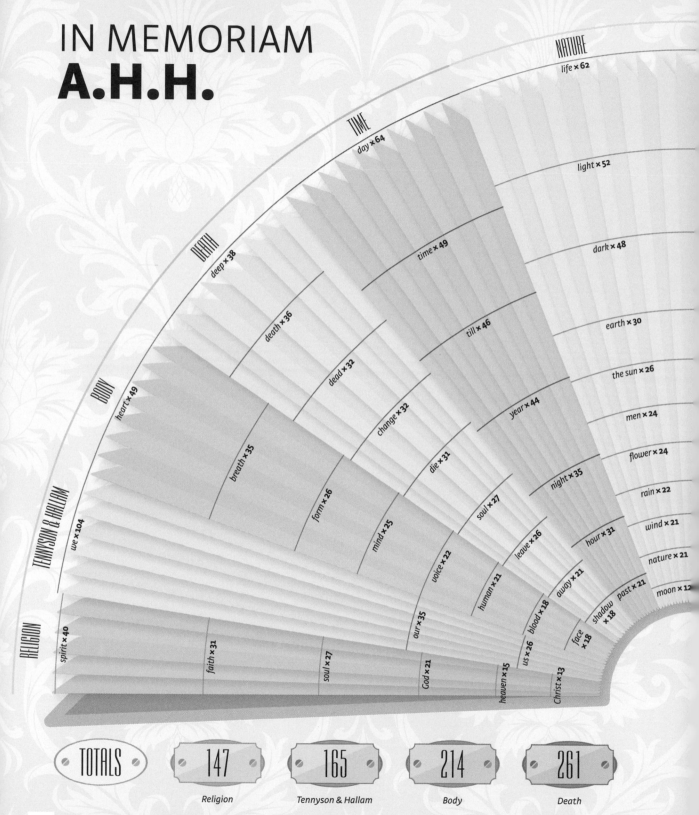

NATURE
life × 62
light × 52
dark × 48
earth × 30
the sun × 26
men × 24
flower × 24
rain × 22
wind × 21
nature × 21
moon × 12

TIME
day × 64
time × 49
till × 46
year × 44
night × 35
hour × 31
away × 21
past × 21

DEATH
deep × 38
death × 36
dead × 32
change × 32
die × 31
soul × 27
leave × 26
blood × 18
shadow × 18
face × 18

BODY
heart × 49
breath × 35
form × 26
mind × 25
voice × 22
human × 21
us × 26

TENNYSON & HALLAM
we × 104
our × 35
heaven × 15
Christ × 13

RELIGION
spirit × 40
faith × 31
soul × 27
God × 21

TOTALS

147	165	214	261
Religion	*Tennyson & Hallam*	*Body*	*Death*

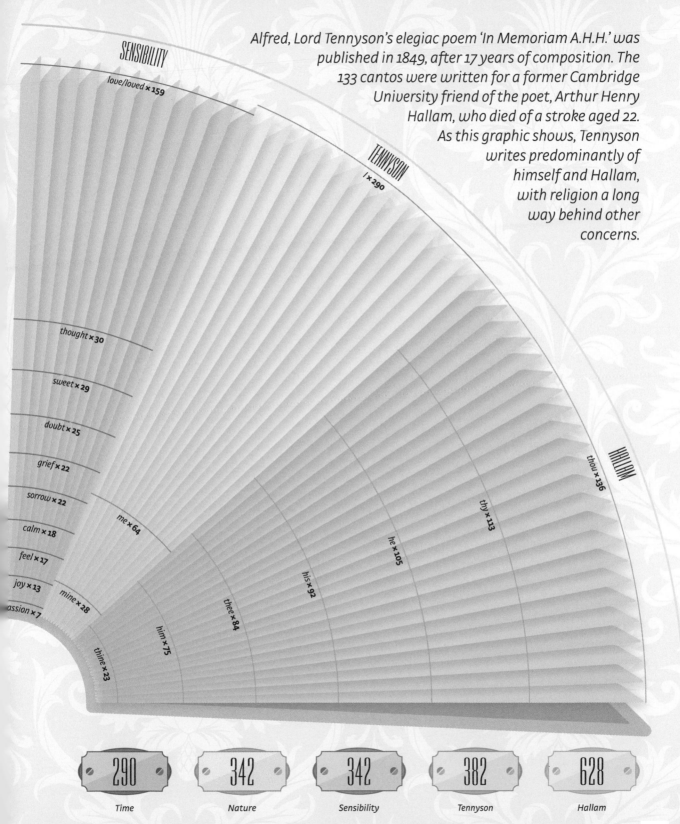

SENSIBILITY

love/loved × 159

TENNYSON

I × 290

thought × 30

sweet × 29

doubt × 25

grief × 22

sorrow × 22

calm × 18

me × 64

feel × 17

joy × 13

...assion × 7

mine × 28

thine × 23

him × 75

thee × 84

his × 92

he × 105

thy × 113

thou × 136

HALLAM

Alfred, Lord Tennyson's elegiac poem 'In Memoriam A.H.H.' was published in 1849, after 17 years of composition. The 133 cantos were written for a former Cambridge University friend of the poet, Arthur Henry Hallam, who died of a stroke aged 22. As this graphic shows, Tennyson writes predominantly of himself and Hallam, with religion a long way behind other concerns.

290	342	342	382	628
Time	Nature	Sensibility	Tennyson	Hallam

DEGREES OF SEPARATION:
STEPHEN KING

At the height of his success, best-selling author Stephen King had been heard to comment that the style of novels he was best known for had as much literary worth as those of the renowned giants of fiction. As this graphic shows, he is only six degrees of separation from some of the greatest writers ever.

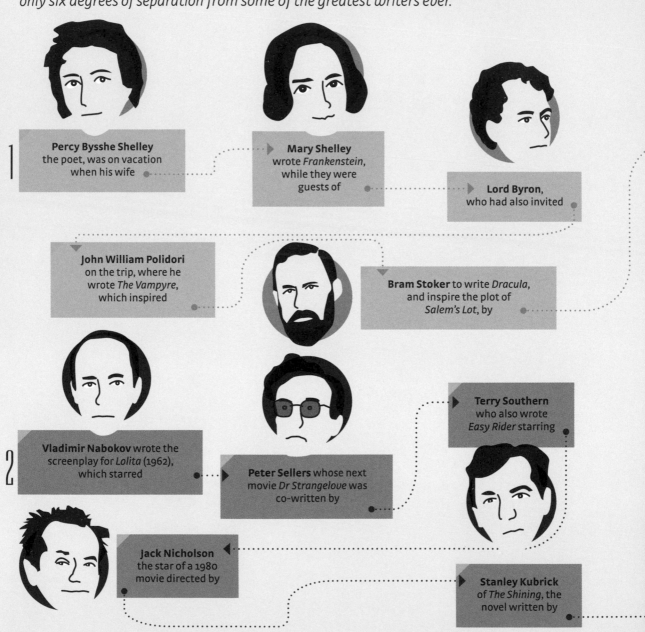

1

Percy Bysshe Shelley the poet, was on vacation when his wife

Mary Shelley wrote *Frankenstein*, while they were guests of

Lord Byron, who had also invited

John William Polidori on the trip, where he wrote *The Vampyre*, which inspired

Bram Stoker to write *Dracula*, and inspire the plot of *Salem's Lot*, by

2

Vladimir Nabokov wrote the screenplay for *Lolita* (1962), which starred

Peter Sellers whose next movie *Dr Strangelove* was co-written by

Terry Southern who also wrote *Easy Rider* starring

Jack Nicholson the star of a 1980 movie directed by

Stanley Kubrick of *The Shining*, the novel written by

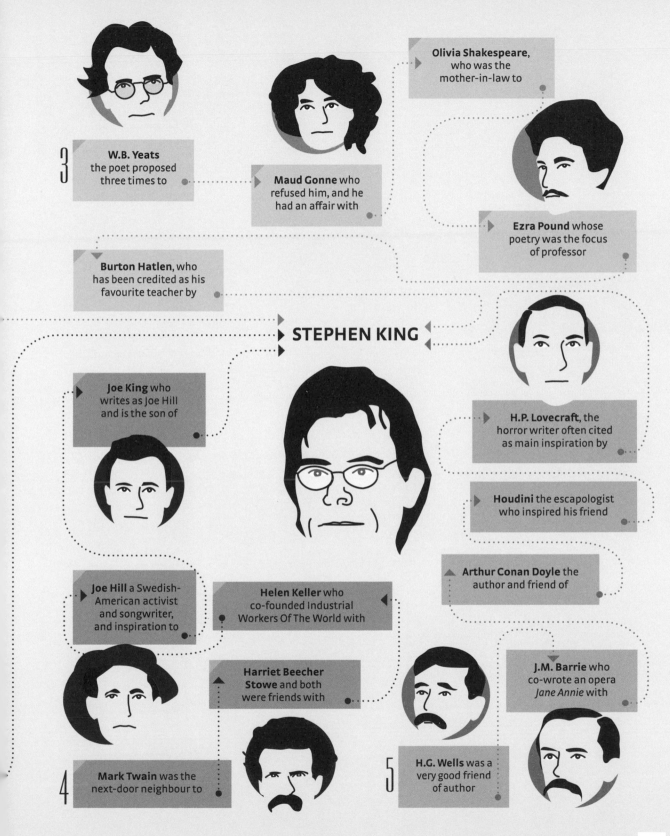

3

W.B. Yeats the poet proposed three times to

Maud Gonne who refused him, and he had an affair with

Olivia Shakespeare, who was the mother-in-law to

Ezra Pound whose poetry was the focus of professor

Burton Hatlen, who has been credited as his favourite teacher by

STEPHEN KING

Joe King who writes as Joe Hill and is the son of

H.P. Lovecraft, the horror writer often cited as main inspiration by

Houdini the escapologist who inspired his friend

Arthur Conan Doyle the author and friend of

Joe Hill a Swedish-American activist and songwriter, and inspiration to

Helen Keller who co-founded Industrial Workers Of The World with

J.M. Barrie who co-wrote an opera *Jane Annie* with

Harriet Beecher Stowe and both were friends with

4

Mark Twain was the next-door neighbour to

5

H.G. Wells was a very good friend of author

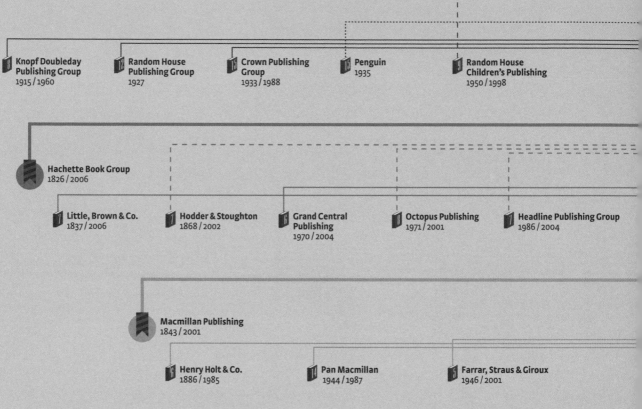

Knopf Doubleday Publishing Group
1915 / 1960

Random House Publishing Group
1927

Crown Publishing Group
1933 / 1988

Penguin
1935

Random House Children's Publishing
1950 / 1998

Hachette Book Group
1826 / 2006

Little, Brown & Co.
1837 / 2006

Hodder & Stoughton
1868 / 2002

Grand Central Publishing
1970 / 2004

Octopus Publishing
1971 / 2001

Headline Publishing Group
1986 / 2004

Macmillan Publishing
1843 / 2001

Henry Holt & Co.
1886 / 1985

Pan Macmillan
1944 / 1987

Farrar, Straus & Giroux
1946 / 2001

A BRIEF HISTORY OF THE BIG FIVE
PUBLISHING COMPANIES

The world's major publishing companies are run by five separate and different media conglomerates. Here's who they are, which publishing houses they own and how many different imprints each has.

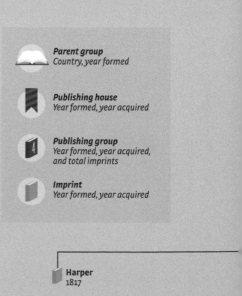

Parent group
Country, year formed

Publishing house
Year formed, year acquired

Publishing group
Year formed, year acquired, and total imprints

Imprint
Year formed, year acquired

Harper
1817

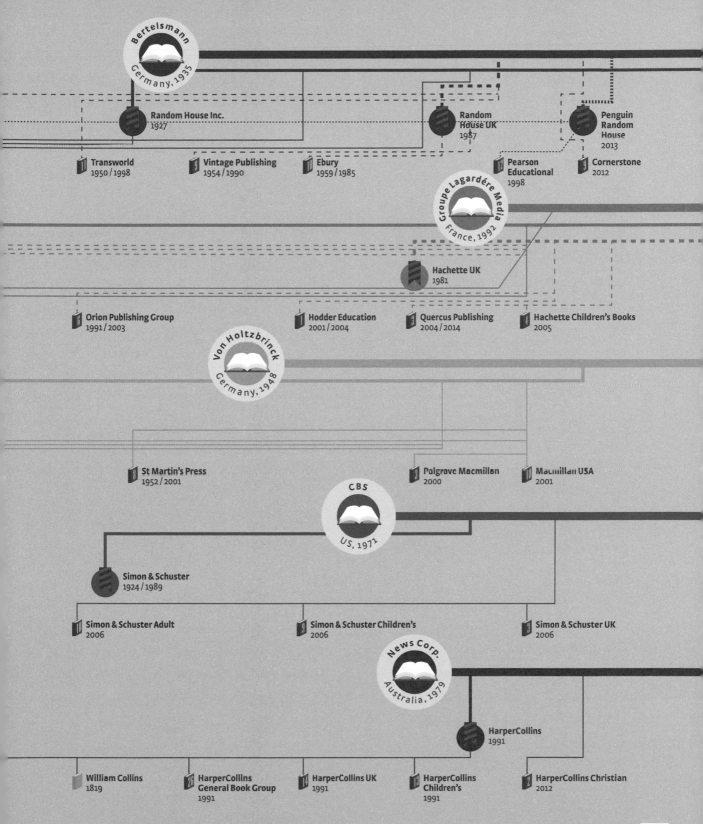

Bertelsmann
Germany, 1935

Random House Inc.
1927

Random House UK
1987

Penguin Random House
2013

Transworld
1950 / 1998

Vintage Publishing
1954 / 1990

Ebury
1959 / 1985

Pearson Educational
1998

Cornerstone
2012

Groupe Lagardére Media
France, 1992

Hachette UK
1981

Orion Publishing Group
1991 / 2003

Hodder Education
2001 / 2004

Quercus Publishing
2004 / 2014

Hachette Children's Books
2005

Von Holtzbrinck
Germany, 1948

St Martin's Press
1952 / 2001

Palgrave Macmillan
2000

Macmillan USA
2001

CBS
US, 1971

Simon & Schuster
1924 / 1989

Simon & Schuster Adult
2006

Simon & Schuster Children's
2006

Simon & Schuster UK
2006

News Corp.
Australia, 1979

HarperCollins
1991

William Collins
1819

HarperCollins General Book Group
1991

HarperCollins UK
1991

HarperCollins Children's
1991

HarperCollins Christian
2012

<table>
<tr>
<td>

1781

CRITIQUE OF PURE REASON

Immanuel Kant

ONTOLOGY

</td>
<td>

1869

CULTURE AND ANARCHY

Matthew Arnold

LITERARY CRITICISM

</td>
<td>

1899

THE INTERPRETATION OF DREAMS

Sigmund Freud

PSYCHOANALYSIS

</td>
<td>

1914

INTRODUCTION TO THE STUDY OF LANGUAGE

Leonard Bloomfield

STRUCTURAL LINGUISTICS

</td>
</tr>
</table>

The nature of being

Methodology of the study of literature

Human mental development

Syntagmatic and paradigmatic analysis

<table>
<tr>
<td>

1936

THE WORK OF ART IN THE AGE OF MECHANICAL REPRODUCTION

Walter Benjamin

PHILOSOPHY OF TECHNOLOGY

</td>
<td>

1956

FUNDAMENTALS OF LANGUAGE

Roman Jakobson

STRUCTURALISM

</td>
<td>

1963

CULTURE AND SOCIETY

Raymond Williams

MARXIST

</td>
<td>

1967

DEATH OF THE AUTHOR

Roland Barthes

POST-STRUCTURALISM

</td>
</tr>
</table>

The nature of technology and social effects

Structural analysis of language

Interpreting texts through Marxist theory

Mediation between concrete reality and abstraction

<table>
<tr>
<td>

1977

THE MODES OF MODERN WRITING

David Lodge

LITERARY THEORY

</td>
<td>

1978

THE ACT OF READING: A THEORY OF AESTHETIC RESPONSE

Wolfgang Iser

RECEPTION THEORY

</td>
<td>

1990

GENDER TROUBLE: FEMINISM AND THE SUBVERSION OF IDENTITY

Judith Butler

FEMINIST THEORY

</td>
<td>

1990

EPISTEMOLOGY OF THE CLOSET

Eve Kosofsky Sedgwick

QUEER THEORY

</td>
</tr>
</table>

The nature of literature

Reader response to text

Feminist-based reading of texts

Post-structuralist reading of queer interpretations of text

1916

COURS DE LINGUISTIQUE GÉNÉRALE

Ferdinand de Saussure

SEMIOTICS

Signs, signifiers and the signified

1927

BEING AND TIME

Martin Heidegger

EXISTENTIAL PHENOMENOLOGY

Being

1928

THE PRINCIPLES OF LITERARY CRITICISM

I.A. Richards

NEW CRITICISM

Close reading of texts (sustained interpretation of brief passages)

1928

ON THE PHENOMENOLOGY OF THE CONSCIOUSNESS OF INTERNAL TIME

Edmund Husserl

PHENOMENOLOGY

Experience and consciousness

1967

VALIDITY IN INTERPRETATION

E.D. Hirsch Jr.

HERMENEUTICS

Interpreting text by historical retrieval of context

1967

OF GRAMMATOLOGY

Jacques Derrida

DECONSTRUCTION

Metaphysics of presence

1975

THE DIALOGIC IMAGINATION

Mikhail Bakhtin

PHILOSOPHY OF LANGUAGE

The nature of meaning, language use, cognition, language and reality

1976–1984

THE HISTORY OF SEXUALITY

Michel Foucault

POST-MODERNISM

Elusive definition of text, non-conformist principles of structure

EVERYONE'S A **CRITIC**

With open access on bookselling websites for people to 'review' a title, everyone can be a critic. Very few of us, however, have been trained to do it. In case you're thinking of getting serious about literary criticism, here's a handy guide to the main schools of criticism, their leading critics and the major philosophical schools that inform much of the theory.

  Theory   Philosophy

● Switzerland   ● Germany   ● Wales   ● France   ● USA   ● England   ● Russia

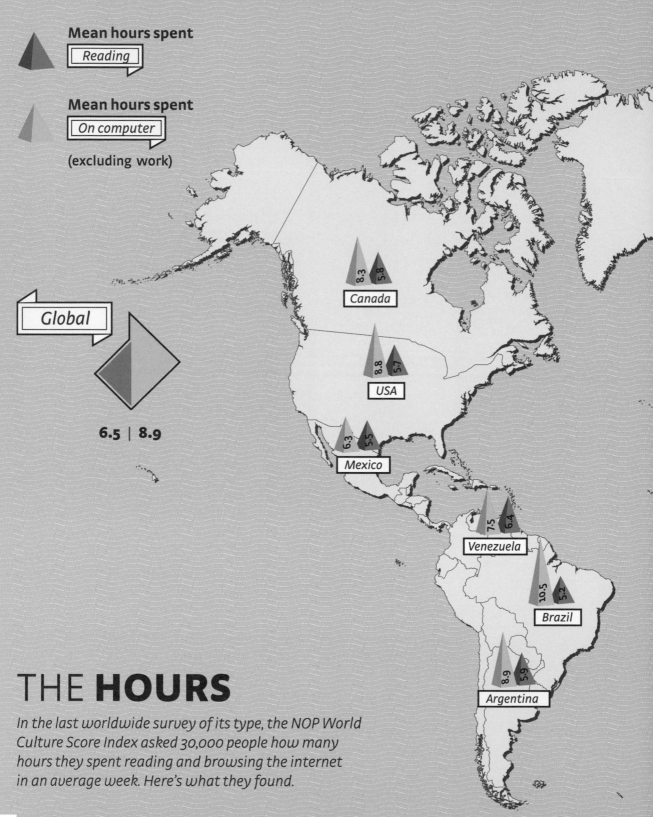

Mean hours spent *Reading*

Mean hours spent *On computer* (excluding work)

Global

6.5 | 8.9

Canada 8.3 | 5.8

USA 8.8 | 5.7

Mexico 6.3 | 5.5

Venezuela 7.5 | 6.4

Brazil 10.5 | 5.2

Argentina 8.9 | 5.9

THE **HOURS**

In the last worldwide survey of its type, the NOP World Culture Score Index asked 30,000 people how many hours they spent reading and browsing the internet in an average week. Here's what they found.

THE **THRILLER** STARTER KIT

Of all the genres favoured by self-published authors, the thriller is most popular. But how to get started? Here is a formula to find a title, names of the main characters and even the self-publishing imprint. The rest is up to your imagination.

Your book title
☐ **+** ☐ **+** ☐

Your main protagonist's first name and occupation
☐ **+** ☐

Your main villain's first name and occupation
☐ **+** ☐

Your self-publishing imprint name
☐ **+** ☐ **+** ☐

SELECT MONTH OF YOUR BIRTH DATE Title link (if needed)
SELECT CURRENT MONTH Protagonist's first name
SELECT MONTH OF YOUR BIRTH DATE Villain's first name

SELECT MONTH OF YOUR BIRTH DATE Imprint first word
SELECT CURRENT MONTH Imprint second word
SELECT MONTH OF PUBLICATION Imprint third word

JANUARY
- In
- Ⓜ Adam **or** Ⓕ Eve
- Ⓜ no name **or** Ⓕ Helen
- Black
- Tarantula
- Books

FEBRUARY
- To
- Ⓜ Jack **or** Ⓕ Jill
- Ⓜ Butler **or** Ⓕ Annie
- Red
- Lizard
- Press

MARCH
- If
- Ⓜ Kurt **or** Ⓕ Saga
- Ⓜ King **or** Ⓕ Alex
- Green
- Panther
- Publishing

APRIL
- The
- Ⓜ Mike **or** Ⓕ Betty
- Ⓜ Self **or** Ⓕ Medea
- Blue
- Crow
- Mysteries

MAY
- Not
- Ⓜ Ford **or** Ⓕ Berlin
- Ⓜ Smith **or** Ⓕ Lee
- Violet
- Vulture
- Stories

JUNE
- So
- Ⓜ Harry **or** Ⓕ Cassandra
- Ⓜ Riuchi **or** Ⓕ Glenn
- Crimson
- Marmoset
- Library

JULY
- Of
- Ⓜ Chance **or** Ⓕ Cordelia
- Ⓜ Henry **or** Ⓕ Nurse 'x'
- Purple
- Swan
- Collection

AUGUST
- From
- Ⓜ Simeon **or** Ⓕ Antigone
- Ⓜ Price **or** Ⓕ Mrs X
- Orange
- Shark
- Corps.

SEPTEMBER
- And
- Ⓜ Hermes **or** Ⓕ P.D.
- Ⓜ Daddy **or** Ⓕ Mamma
- Grey
- Mosquito
- House

OCTOBER
- But
- Ⓜ Josef **or** Ⓕ Lissy
- Ⓜ Kurt **or** Ⓕ Cruella
- Pink
- Arachnid
- Series

NOVEMBER
- Have
- Ⓜ Siggi **or** Ⓕ Frankie
- Ⓜ H **or** Ⓕ E
- Lime
- Wolf
- & Co.

DECEMBER
- As
- Ⓜ Ulysses **or** Ⓕ Molly
- Ⓜ Yussuf **or** Ⓕ Betty
- White
- Dog
- Brothers

SUNDAY	MONDAY	TUESDAY	WEDNESDAY	THURSDAY	FRIDAY	SATURDAY
SELECT YOUR BIRTH DATE — Single title or first word **SELECT TODAY'S DATE** — Predicative adjective for the title **DAY OF THE WEEK (TODAY'S DATE)** — Protagonist's occupation **DAY OF THE WEEK (YOUR BIRTH DATE)** — Villain's occupation			**1** — Caught / Sleep / Police / Police	**2** — Return / Blood / Lawyer / Organized crime employee	**3** — Fatal / Rain / Coroner / Psychopath or sociopath	**4** — Forget / Time / Private detective / Cyber criminal
5 — Memory / Home / Armed forces (or ex-) / PTS sufferer	**6** — Echo / Forlorn / Ex-elite military or federal police / Ex-lover	**7** — Outside / Run / Average civilian / Celebrity with a secret	**8** — Cry / Hell / Police / Police	**9** — Gone / Past / Lawyer / Organized crime employee	**10** — Still / Them / Coroner / Psychopath or sociopath	**11** — Cold / Away / Private detective / Cyber criminal
12 — Found / Forgotten / Armed forces (or ex-) / PTS sufferer	**13** — Child / Rules / Ex-elite military or federal police / Ex-lover	**14** — Storm / Place / Average civilian / Celebrity with a secret	**15** — Fall / Money / Police / Police	**16** — Just / Grave / Lawyer / Organized crime employee	**17** — Boy / Eyes / Coroner / Psychopath or sociopath	**18** — Long / Chance / Private detective / Cyber criminal
19 — Little / Nothing / Armed forces (or ex-) / PTS sufferer	**20** — Final / Beloved / Ex-elite military or federal police / Ex-lover	**21** — Naked / Hole / Average civilian / Celebrity with a secret	**22** — Girl / Disappeared / Police / Police	**23** — Fear / When / Lawyer / Organized crime employee	**24** — Believe / Heaven / Coroner / Psychopath or sociopath	**25** — Back / Here / Private detective / Cyber criminal
26 — Blind / Them / Armed forces (or ex-) / PTS sufferer	**27** — Missing / Ending / Ex-elite military or federal police / Ex-lover	**28** — Shame / Song / Average civilian / Celebrity with a secret	**29** — Watch / Forever / Police / Police	**30** — Losing / Time / Lawyer / Organized crime employee	**31** — Thirteen / Again / Coroner / Psychopath or sociopath	THE END

135

BIG SCREEN **WRITERS**

★ REAL AUTHOR ★

box office	$1m	$1.65m	$2.2m
REAL AUTHOR MOVIE & YEAR	**T.S. Eliot** (1888–1965, USA) *Tom And Viv* (1994)	**Joe Orton** (1933–1967, England) *Prick Up Your Ears* (1987)	**Oscar Wilde** (1854–1900, Ireland) *Wilde* (1998)

$2.9m	$4.2m	$6.1m	$10.9m
Sylvia Plath (1932– 1963, USA), **Ted Hughes** (1930–1998, England) *Sylvia (2003)*	**Dorothy Parker** (1893–1967, USA) *Mrs Parker And The Vicious Circle* (1994)	**Knut Hamsun** (1859–1952, Norway) *Hamsun* (1996)	**Jean-Baptiste Poquelin (aka Molière)** (1622–1673, France) *Molière* (2007)

$14.4m	$16.15m	$23.5m	$35m
John Keats (1795–1821, England) *Bright Star* (2009)	**Iris Murdoch** (1919–1999, Ireland) *Iris* (2001)	**Henry Miller** (1891–1980, USA), **Anaïs Nin** (1903–1977, France) *Henry & June (1990)*	**Beatrix Potter** (1866–1943, England) *Miss Potter* (2006)

$49.2m	$109m	$112.5m	$289.3m
Truman Capote (1924–1984, USA) *Capote* (2005)	**Virginia Woolf** (1882–1941, England) *The Hours* (2002)	**P.L. Travers** (1899–1996, Australia) *Saving Mr Banks* (2013)	**William Shakespeare** (1582–1616, England) *Shakespeare In Love* (1998)

So-called 'serious' writers have usually disdained Hollywood and movies in general, but that hasn't stopped movie-makers from using them as lead characters. But what do the movie-going public prefer, biopics of real authors, or movies about fictional authors? Here's a comparison between some of the best-known in both camps, and their box office success.

★ FICTIONAL AUTHOR ★

box office ▶

FICTIONAL AUTHOR MOVIE & YEAR

$1.5m ▶
Jon Holt
crime fiction
Insomnia
(1998)

$1.5m ▶
Walter Kranz
poet
Satansbraten
(1976)

$4.9m ▶
Andrew Wyke
crime fiction
Sleuth
(2007)

$11.1m ▶
Bernard Berkman
fiction
The Squid And The Whale (2005)

$12m ▶
Barton Fink
playwright
Barton Fink
(1991)

$15.4m ▶
Edward De Vere
playwright, poet
Anonymous
(2011)

$16m ▶
Harry Block
fiction
Deconstructing Harry
(1997)

$24m ▶
Dexter Cornell
non-fiction
D.O.A.
(1988)

$33.5m ▶
Grady Tripp
non-fiction
Wonder Boys
(2000)

$60.2m ▶
'The ghost writer'
non-fiction
The Ghost Writer
(2010)

$75m ▶
Jack Torrance
fiction
The Shining
(1980)

$77.5m ▶
Georg Dreyman
playwright
The Lives Of Others
(2006)

$120m ▶
Paul Sheldon
crime fiction
Misery
(1990)

$315m ▶
Melvin Udall
fiction
As Good As It Gets
(1997)

$353m ▶
Catherine Trammell
crime fiction
Basic Instinct
(1992)

BEAT HAPPENINGS

With the opening of the City Lights bookstore in San Francisco, the Beat Generation had a base from which to conquer the world with their jazz-inflected poetry and prose. Here are the main Beat happenings, the Beats and their key works.

City Lights – bookstore opening, 1953

261 Columbus Avenue,
San Francisco, CA

- ● *City Lights* magazine, 1952
- △ ● *A Coney Island Of The Mind*, 1958
- ● Manager City Lights Pocket Bookstore, 1953–1976
- ● Editor *City Lights* magazine and books, executive director, 1971–2007

Howl obscenity trial, 1957

Municipal Court,
San Francisco, CA

Reading at the Six Gallery, 1955

261 Columbus Avenue,
San Francisco, CA

- ● Artist and co-owner of Six Gallery, 1954–1965
- △ ● *Ekstasis*, 1959
- △ ● *On Bear's Head*, 1960
- △ ● *Turtle Island*, 1974
- △ ● *The New Book/A Book Of Torture*, 1961
- △ ● *Howl*, 1955

- ● Peter D. Martin (1923–1988)
- ● Lawrence Ferlinghetti (1919–2021)
- ● Shig Murao (1926–1999)
- ● Nancy Joyce Peters (1936–)
- ● Wally Hendrick (1928–2003)
- ● Philip Lamantia (1927–2005)
- ● Philip Whalen (1923–2002)
- ● Gary Snyder (1934–)
- ● Michael McLure (1932–2020)
- ● Allen Ginsberg (1927–1997)
- ● Judge Clayton W. Horn (1904–1981)
- ● Gilbert Millstein (1915–1999)
- ● Jack Kerouac (1922–1969)

- ● Neal Cassady (1926–1968)
- ● Peter Orlovsky (1933–2010)
- ● William S. Burroughs (1914–1997)
- ● Gregory Corso (1930–2001)
- ● Harold Norse (1916–2009)
- ● Brion Gysin (1916–1986, UK)
- ● Ian Sommerville (1940–1976, UK)
- ● Adrian Mitchell (1932–2008, UK)
- ● Alexander Trocchi (1925–1984, UK)
- ● Anselm Hollo (1934–2013, Finland)
- ● Michael Horovitz (1935–2021, UK)
- ● Simon Vinkenoog (1928–2009, Netherlands)

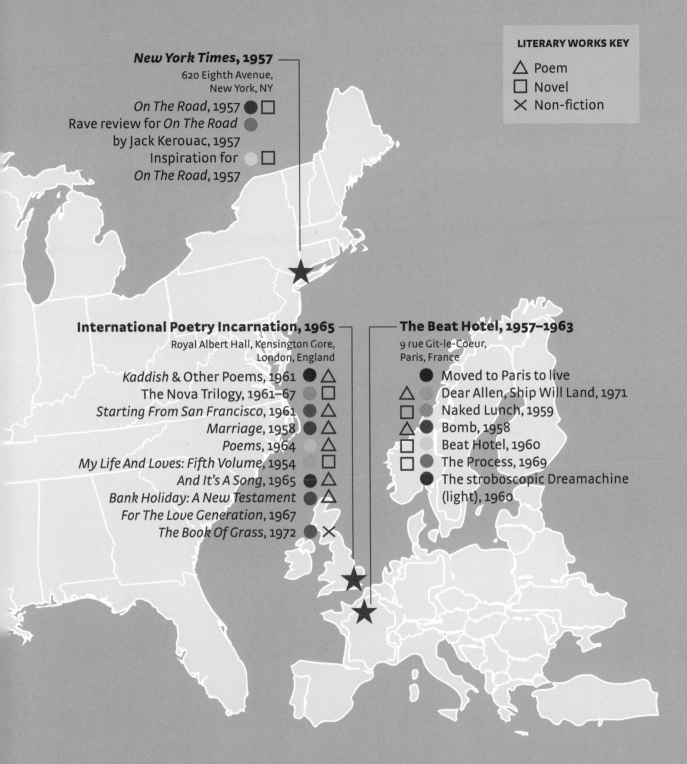

LITERARY WORKS KEY

△ Poem
□ Novel
✕ Non-fiction

New York Times, 1957

620 Eighth Avenue,
New York, NY

On The Road, 1957 ● □
Rave review for *On The Road* ●
by Jack Kerouac, 1957
Inspiration for ○ □
On The Road, 1957

International Poetry Incarnation, 1965

Royal Albert Hall, Kensington Gore,
London, England

Kaddish & *Other Poems*, 1961 ● △
The Nova Trilogy, 1961–67 ● □
Starting From San Francisco, 1961 ● △
Marriage, 1958 ● △
Poems, 1964 ○ △
My Life And Loves: Fifth Volume, 1954 ● □
And It's A Song, 1965 ● △
Bank Holiday: A New Testament ● △
For The Love Generation, 1967
The Book Of Grass, 1972 ● ✕

The Beat Hotel, 1957–1963

9 rue Git-le-Coeur,
Paris, France

● Moved to Paris to live
△ Dear Allen, Ship Will Land, 1971
□ Naked Lunch, 1959
△ Bomb, 1958
□ Beat Hotel, 1960
□ The Process, 1969
● The stroboscopic Dreamachine
(light), 1960

BOYS WILL BE **GIRLS**

Sometimes it's hard to be a woman. Or a man. Authors who have chosen to write under a pseudonym of the opposite gender have done so for a variety of reasons, but is there one rule for boys and another for girls?

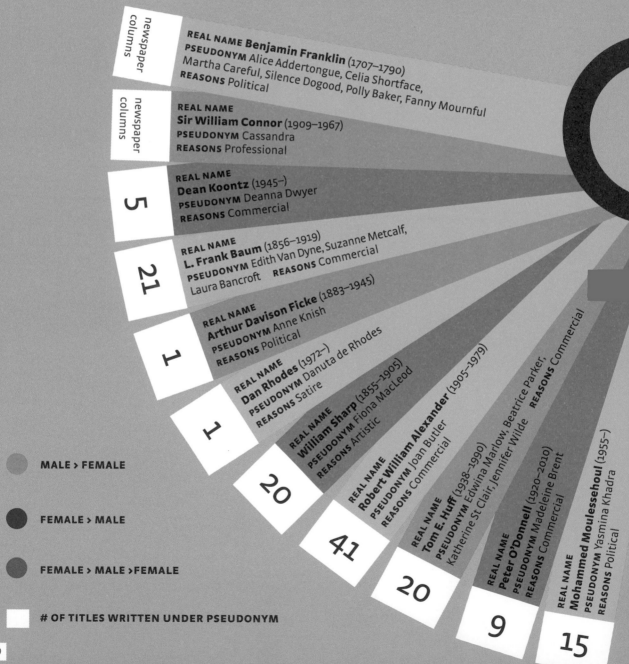

newspaper columns
REAL NAME Benjamin Franklin (1707–1790)
PSEUDONYM Alice Addertongue, Celia Shortface, Martha Careful, Silence Dogood, Polly Baker, Fanny Mournful
REASONS Political

newspaper columns
REAL NAME Sir William Connor (1909–1967)
PSEUDONYM Cassandra
REASONS Professional

5
REAL NAME Dean Koontz (1945–)
PSEUDONYM Deanna Dwyer
REASONS Commercial

5 21
REAL NAME L. Frank Baum (1856–1919)
PSEUDONYM Edith Van Dyne, Suzanne Metcalf, Laura Bancroft
REASONS Commercial

1
REAL NAME Arthur Davison Ficke (1883–1945)
PSEUDONYM Anne Knish
REASONS Political

1
REAL NAME Dan Rhodes (1972–)
PSEUDONYM Danuta de Rhodes
REASONS Satire

20
REAL NAME William Sharp (1855–1905)
PSEUDONYM Fiona MacLeod
REASONS Artistic

41
REAL NAME Robert William Alexander (1905–1979)
PSEUDONYM Joan Butler
REASONS Commercial

20
REAL NAME Tom E. Huff (1938–1990)
PSEUDONYM Edwina Marlow, Beatrice Parker, Katherine St Clair, Jennifer Wilde
REASONS Commercial

9
REAL NAME Peter O'Donnell (1920–2010)
PSEUDONYM Madeleine Brent
REASONS Commercial

15
REAL NAME Mohammed Moulessehoul (1955–)
PSEUDONYM Yasmina Khadra
REASONS Political

● **MALE > FEMALE**

● **FEMALE > MALE**

● **FEMALE > MALE > FEMALE**

☐ **# OF TITLES WRITTEN UNDER PSEUDONYM**

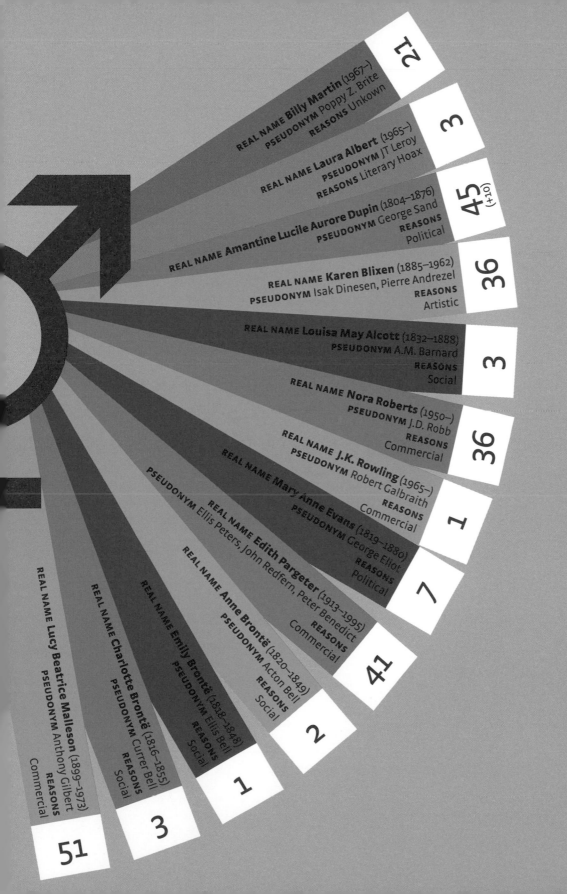

REAL NAME **Billy Martin** (1967–)
PSEUDONYM Poppy Z. Brite
REASONS Unkown

27

REAL NAME **Laura Albert** (1965–)
PSEUDONYM JT Leroy
REASONS Literary Hoax

3

REAL NAME **Amantine Lucile Aurore Dupin** (1804–1876)
PSEUDONYM George Sand
REASONS Political

45 (+10)

REAL NAME **Karen Blixen** (1885–1962)
PSEUDONYM Isak Dinesen, Pierre Andrezel
REASONS Artistic

36

REAL NAME **Louisa May Alcott** (1832–1888)
PSEUDONYM A.M. Barnard
REASONS Social

3

REAL NAME **Nora Roberts** (1950–)
PSEUDONYM J.D. Robb
REASONS Commercial

36

REAL NAME **J.K. Rowling** (1965–)
PSEUDONYM Robert Galbraith
REASONS Commercial

1

REAL NAME **Mary Anne Evans** (1819–1880)
PSEUDONYM George Eliot
REASONS Political

7

REAL NAME **Edith Pargeter** (1913–1995)
PSEUDONYM Ellis Peters, John Redfern, Peter Benedict
REASONS Commercial

41

REAL NAME **Anne Brontë** (1820–1849)
PSEUDONYM Acton Bell
REASONS Social

2

REAL NAME **Emily Brontë** (1818–1848)
PSEUDONYM Ellis Bell
REASONS Social

1

REAL NAME **Charlotte Brontë** (1816–1855)
PSEUDONYM Currer Bell
REASONS Social

3

REAL NAME **Lucy Beatrice Malleson** (1899–1973)
PSEUDONYM Anthony Gilbert
REASONS Commercial

51

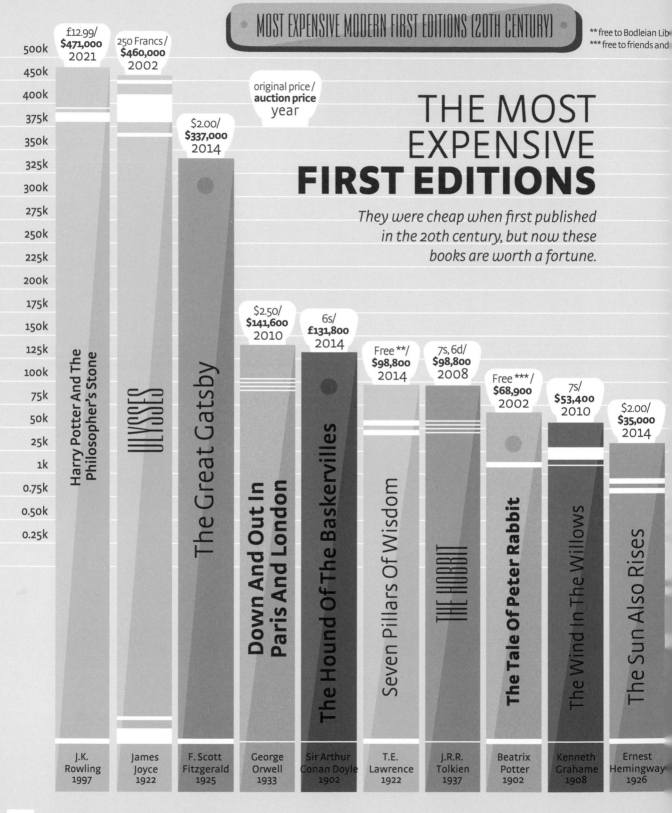

THE MOST EXPENSIVE
FIRST EDITIONS

They were cheap when first published in the 20th century, but now these books are worth a fortune.

original price / **auction price** year

£12.99/ $471,000 2021

250 Francs / $460,000 2002

$2.00/ $337,000 2014

$2.50/ $141,600 2010

6s/ £131,800 2014

Free ** / $98,800 2014

7s, 6d/ $98,800 2008

Free * / $68,900** 2002

7s/ $53,400 2010

$2.00/ $35,000 2014

500k
450k
400k
375k
350k
325k
300k
275k
250k
225k
200k
175k
150k
125k
100k
75k
50k
25k
1k
0.75k
0.50k
0.25k

Harry Potter And The Philosopher's Stone

ULYSSES

The Great Gatsby

Down And Out In Paris And London

The Hound Of The Baskervilles

Seven Pillars Of Wisdom

THE HOBBIT

The Tale Of Peter Rabbit

The Wind In The Willows

The Sun Also Rises

| J.K. Rowling 1997 | James Joyce 1922 | F. Scott Fitzgerald 1925 | George Orwell 1933 | Sir Arthur Conan Doyle 1902 | T.E. Lawrence 1922 | J.R.R. Tolkien 1937 | Beatrix Potter 1902 | Kenneth Grahame 1908 | Ernest Hemingway 1926 |

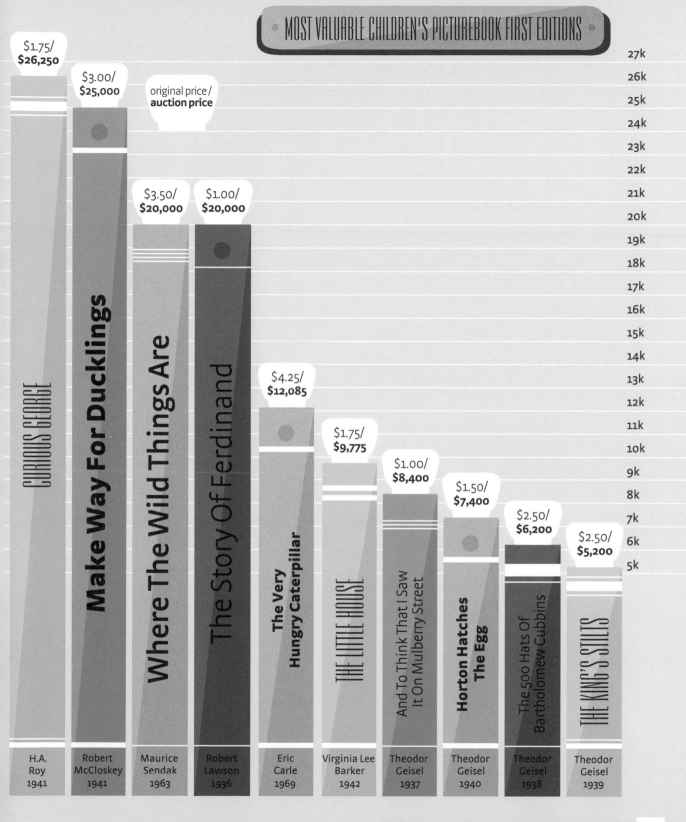

MOST VALUABLE CHILDREN'S PICTUREBOOK FIRST EDITIONS

$1.75/
$26,250

$3.00/
$25,000

original price /
auction price

$3.50/
$20,000

$1.00/
$20,000

$4.25/
$12,085

$1.75/
$9,775

$1.00/
$8,400

$1.50/
$7,400

$2.50/
$6,200

$2.50/
$5,200

CURIOUS GEORGE

Make Way For Ducklings

Where The Wild Things Are

The Story Of Ferdinand

The Very
Hungry Caterpillar

THE LITTLE HOUSE

And To Think That I Saw
It On Mulberry Street

Horton Hatches
The Egg

The 500 Hats Of
Bartholomew Cubbins

THE KING'S STILTS

| H.A. Roy 1941 | Robert McCloskey 1941 | Maurice Sendak 1963 | Robert Lawson 1936 | Eric Carle 1969 | Virginia Lee Barker 1942 | Theodor Geisel 1937 | Theodor Geisel 1940 | Theodor Geisel 1938 | Theodor Geisel 1939 |

27k
26k
25k
24k
23k
22k
21k
20k
19k
18k
17k
16k
15k
14k
13k
12k
11k
10k
9k
8k
7k
6k
5k

Henry James

1843 **USA**

1916 **England**

England 1876 / Personal

18*

Portrait Of A Lady (1880)

Thomas Mann

1875 **Germany**

1955 **Switzerland**

Switzerland 1933 / Political
USA 1939 / Political
Switzerland 1952 / Personal

5

Lotte In Weimar:
The Beloved Returns (1939)

James Joyce

1882 **Ireland**

1941 **Switzerland**

Austria-Hungary 1904 / Professional
Switzerland 1915 / Professional
France 1920 / Personal
Zurich 1940 / Political

5

Ulysses (1922)

Vladimir Nabokov

1899 **Russia**

1977 **Switzerland**

Ukraine 1917 / Political
England 1919 / Political
Germany 1922 / Professional
France 1937 / Political
USA 1940 / Political
Switzerland 1961 / Personal

18*

Ada Or Ardor:
A Family Chronicle (1969)

V.S. Naipaul

1932 **Trinidad**

–

England 1950 / Educational

14

A Bend In The River (1979)

Salman Rushdie

1947 **India**

–

England 1958 / Educational
USA 2000 / Commercial

14*

The Satanic Verses (1988)

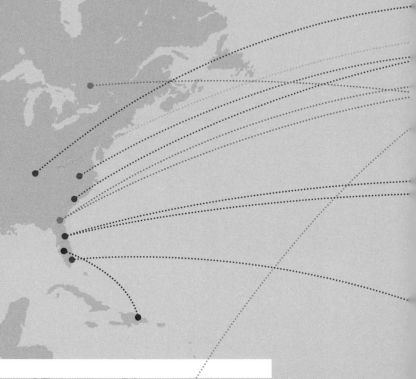

EXILE'S **KINGDOM**

Literature is peppered with authors who have found an
audience by writing about their homeland from which they
are exiled. Here are arguably the dozen most famous writers
in exile, where they moved to, why, and their key novel.

Mohsin Hamid

1971 **Pakistan**

–

USA 1974–1980 / Personal
USA 1989–2001 / Educational
England 2001–2009 /
Professional

3

(A)

*The Reluctant
Fundamentalist* (2007)

Chimamanda Ngozi Adichie

1977 **Nigeria**

–

USA 1996 / Educational

3*

(A)

Half Of A Yellow Sun (2006)

Marjane Satrapi

1969 **Iran**

–

Austria 1983–1988 / Political,
Educational
France 1994 / Political

11

(C)

Persepolis (2000)

Rohinton Mistry

1952 **India**

–

Canada 1975 / Educational

6

(C)

Such A Long Journey (1991)

Kiran Desai

1972 **India**

–

England 1985 / Personal
USA 1986 / Educational

2

(N)

The Inheritance Of Loss (2006)

Junot Diaz

1968 **Dominican Republic**

–

USA 1974 / Personal

2*

(N)

*The Brief Wondrous Life
Of Oscar Wao* (2007)

Author
year of birth **country**
emigrated to, when / reason for move
works published in exile
(C) critical / (N) nostalgic / (A) ambiguous about homeland
key work

(* novels only)

LOSE THE NAME OF **ACTION**

Shakespeare's Hamlet has inspired so many literary works, including poetry, plays, movies, songs, novels and criticism, that it is arguably the most inspirational work of literature ever. Here we discover that Act III – and the 'To be or not to be' soliloquy in particular – is by far the most quoted.

Year	Author / Work	Act I	Act II	Act III	Act IV	Act V
1875	Bram Stoker — *Dracula*	💀				
1922	Edith Wharton — *The Glimpses Of The Moon*	💀				
1922	Aldous Huxley — *Mortal Coils*			💀		
1923	David Lloyd George — *Slings And Arrows*			💀		
1930	Graham Greene — *The Name Of Action*			💀		
1933	John Masefield — *Bird Of Dawning*	💀				
1935	Ogden Nash — *The Primrose Path*	💀				
1938	Georgette Heyer — *No Wind Of Blame*				💀	
1947	Louis Auchincloss — *The Indifferent Children*		💀			
1948	Clifford Bax — *Rosemary For Remembrance*				💀	
1952	Agatha Christie — *The Mousetrap*			💀		
1955	Monica Dickens — *The Winds Of Heaven*	💀				
1959	Philip K. Dick — *Time Out Of Joint*	💀				
1966	Tom Stoppard — *Rosencrantz And Guildenstern Are Dead*					💀
1967	Nigel Balchin — *Kings Of Infinite Space*		💀			
1968	Marguerite Duras — *A Sea Of Troubles*			💀		
1969	Richard Yates — *A Special Providence*					💀
1971	D.H. Lawrence — *The Mortal Coil And Other Stories*			💀		
1972	Isaac Asimov — *The Gods Themselves*		💀			
1978	Richard Matheson — *What Dreams May Come*			💀		
1980	Anthony Powell — *Infants Of The Spring*	💀				
1987	Lee Strasberg — *A Dream Of Passion: The Development Of The Method*		💀			
1991	Robert B. Parker — *Perchance To Dream*			💀		
1996	David Foster Wallace — *Infinite Jest*					💀
2004	Jasper Fforde — *Something Rotten*	💀				💀

[of which 'To Be Or Not To Be' soliloquy 8%]

ACT I	ACT II	ACT III	ACT IV	ACT V
24.5%	15.5%	39%	8%	10%

ALL THE **DEAD** YOUR POETS

ALL THE **DEAD** YOUR POETS

*When Keats died of tuberculosis in 1821 aged 25, and Shelley drowned the following year aged 29, it seemed to begin a sad tradition of fiery young poets who lived and loved too much, dying before reaching the age of 40. Here are the greatest since then to have left this earth before their time.**

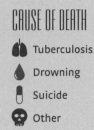

CAUSE OF DEATH

Tuberculosis
Drowning
Suicide
Other

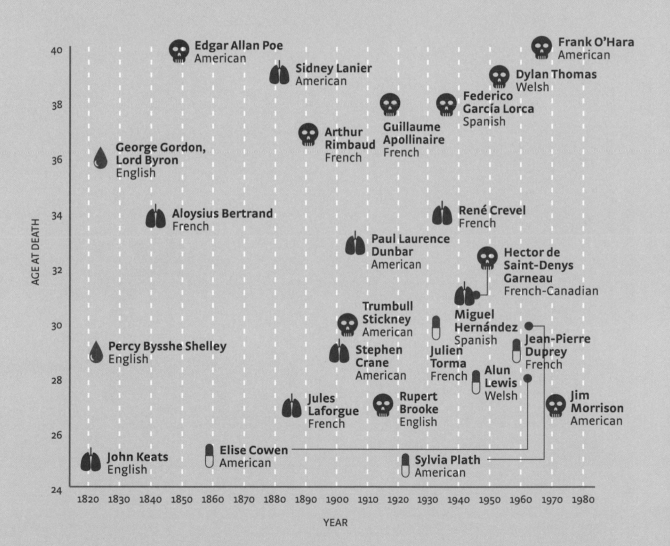

AGE AT DEATH

40 — Edgar Allan Poe, American
Frank O'Hara, American
Sidney Lanier, American
Dylan Thomas, Welsh
38 — Federico García Lorca, Spanish
Arthur Rimbaud, French
Guillaume Apollinaire, French
36 — George Gordon, Lord Byron, English
34 — Aloysius Bertrand, French
René Crevel, French
Paul Laurence Dunbar, American
32 — Hector de Saint-Denys Garneau, French-Canadian
Trumbull Stickney, American
30 — Miguel Hernández, Spanish
Julien Torma, French
Jean-Pierre Duprey, French
Stephen Crane, American
Percy Bysshe Shelley, English
28 — Alun Lewis, Welsh
Jim Morrison, American
Jules Laforgue, French
Rupert Brooke, English
26 — Elise Cowen, American
Sylvia Plath, American
John Keats, English
24 —

YEAR: 1820 1830 1840 1850 1860 1870 1880 1890 1900 1910 1920 1930 1940 1950 1960 1970 1980

* not including those killed in action during wars

DEAR **READER**

You, dear reader, can feel incredibly close to the characters on the page, and perhaps even closer to the person who put them there: the author. As this graphic shows, the dear reader is never more than six degrees away from the writer.

1

Jane Austen had her first two novels published by

Thomas Egerton, *Sense And Sensibility* (1811) and *Mansfield Park* (1813), and they were read by

George IV, then Prince Regent and a fan, who she met in 1815, the year she switched publisher to

John Murray who printed *Emma* (1815), *Persuasion* (1816) and *Northanger Abbey* after her death in 1817, but allowed her work to go out of print in 1820, until

Richard Bentley republished all of Jane Austen's novels in 1832, since when they have remained in print for the pleasure of you,

Louis XVIII who gave him a royal pension, allowing Hugo to write for a living in France, which he did until 1851 when

Napoleon III became emperor of France and Hugo went into exile, where he wrote *Les Misérables*, which was translated into English in 1862 by

2

Victor Hugo began as a poet, and was honoured for his work in 1822 by

Charles Edwin Wilbour an American, whose translation made the novel a hit in the United States, where the first movie of the book was made in 1935 starring

Fredric March as Jean Valjean, renewing the popularity of the novel, which is still available for you,

3

Salman Rushdie began his writing career in advertising, finding success with a slogan for

American Express, before writing *Midnight's Children*, his 1981 novel, voted by

Ayatollah Khomeini, he issued a fatwa on the writer, forcing him into hiding, only emerging for

Malcolm Bradbury and fellow judges of the Booker Prize best of the year, allowing Rushdie time to write *The Satanic Verses* (1988) which so annoyed

Bono, who got him to appear on stage with U2 in 1993, and encouraged Rushdie to carry on writing for you,

Anne Massitte the editor at Vintage who thought it good enough to print millions of copies of three volumes of *Fifty Shades* for you,

Valerie Hoskins a London-based literary agent was hired to construct a deal with major publishing company Random House in New York, via

Raymond Carver; *What I Talk About When I Talk About Running*, one of the best-selling books on running ever, and read by millions of you,

Amanda Hayward whose Australian-based ebook publishing company Writer's Coffee Shop published the first edition of *Fifty Shades*, selling enough copies that

DEAR READER

Franz Kafka titled *Kafka On The Shore* in 2004, and then by a non-fiction work that owed its title to

The Beatles whose song *Norwegian Wood* became the title of one of his best-selling novels in English in 2000, followed by a work inspired by

Stephenie Meyer in her *Twilight* series, and loved by fellow fan-fiction writer

4

Haruki Murakami grew up in Japan reading Western literature, a fan of

Jack Kerouac, listening to the music of

5

E.L. James is the pen name of the author of *Fifty Shades Of Grey* (2011), begun as fan fiction based on characters created by

WHAT'S THE **WEATHER** LIKE?

From Homer to James Herbert via Shakespeare and Victor Hugo, the weather in fiction has played an important part in underpinning a sense of mood, pointing up intention and acting as a metaphor. Here are 40 uses of different types of weather in classics of literature and what they represent.

STORMS

MADNESS
King Lear William Shakespeare (1603–1607)

Wuthering Heights Emily Brontë (1845–46)

EMOTIONAL TURMOIL

Lord Of The Flies William Golding (1954)

VIOLENCE

The Odyssey Homer (8 BCE)

TURMOIL

CHANGE
The Seagull Anton Chekhov (1895)

Les Misérables Victor Hugo (1862)

MALEVOLENT WORLD

Great Expectations Charles Dickens (1861)

DEATH

Jude The Obscure Thomas Hardy (1895)

One Day In The Life Of Ivan Denisovich Aleksandr Solzhenitsyn (1962)

Lord Jim Joseph Conrad (1900)

DISORDER

The Aenid Virgil (19–29 BCE)

RAGE

DEFEAT

SNOW

HOPE
The Lion, The Witch And The Wardrobe C.S. Lewis (1950)

A Farewell To Arms Ernest Hemingway (1929)

LOSS OF HOPE

Ethan Frome Edith Wharton (1911)

DESOLATION

The Dead James Joyce (1914)

ISOLATION

A Child's Christmas In Wales Dylan Thomas (1955)

Andorra Max Frisch (1961)

NOSTALGIA

HIDDEN CRIMES

SUN

Treasure Island
Robert Louis
Stevenson (1883)

DISCONTENT

REBIRTH   TRAGEDY

The Stranger
Albert Camus
(1943)

Death In Venice
Thomas Mann
(1912)

Walden Henry
David Thoreau
(1854)

*The Heart Is A Lonely
Hunter* Carson
McCullers (1940)

DEATH   OPPRESSION   DISEASE

CONTROL

The Plague Albert
Camus (1947)

*A Passage To
India* E.M.
Forster (1924)

*Brave New
World* Aldous
Huxley (1932)

UNREST

RAIN

Ode On Melancholy
John Keats (1819)

JEOPARDY

MELANCHOLIA

Fahrenheit 451
Ray Bradbury
(1953)

*Sense and
Sensibility* Jane
Austen (1811)

*Poisonwood
Bible* Barbara
Kingsolver (1998)

CATHARSIS   *The Grapes Of Wrath*
John Steinbeck (1939)   HOPE

BAPTISM   *The Big Sleep* Raymond
Chandler (1939)   FOREBODING

OPPRESSION

*The Strange Case Of Dr
Jekyll And Mr Hyde* Robert
Louis Stevenson (1886)

*The Fall Of The House
Of Usher* Edgar
Allan Poe (1839)

Bleak House Charles
Dickens (1853)

The Woman In Black
Susan Hill (1983)

FOG   CONFUSION

FOREBODING

Party Going Henry
Green (1939)

PSYCHOSIS

Rebecca Daphne Du
Maurier (1938)

Hamlet William
Shakespeare
(1603-1607)

The Fog James Herbert (1975)

STASIS

A WORLD OF **CRIME**

From London and Los Angeles to Ystad and Botswana, most of the world's popular serial literary detectives, whether police, private or amateur, are synonymous with a particular city. While Miss Marple, Hercule Poirot, Lord Peter Wimsey and Jack Reacher are wanderers, these detectives stay put, by and large.

ENGLAND

UNITED STATES

Sherlock Holmes - 1891–1927
Arthur Conan Doyle, London — 4 | 27

Philo Vance - 1926–1939
S.S. Van Dine, New York — 12

Adam Dalgliesh - 1962–2008
P.D. James, London — 14

Sam Spade - 1930–1932
Dashiell Hammett, San Francisco — 1 | 3

DCI Reg Wexford - 1964–2013
Ruth Rendell, Sussex — 24 | 5

Philip Marlowe - 1939–1958
Raymond Chandler, Los Angeles — 8 | 5

DS Charles Wycliffe - 1968–2000
W.J. Burley, Devon, Cornwall — 22

Mike Hammer - 1947–1997
Mickey Spillane, New York — 13

Inspector Morse - 1975–1999
Colin Dexter, Oxford — 13 | 10

Matt Scudder - 1976–2011
Lawrence Block, New York — 17 | 12

V.I. Warshawski - 1982–2013
Sara Paretsky, Chicago — 21 | 17

Police 🔍 Private 🔍 Amateur 🔍

Harry Bosch - 1992–2021
Michael Connelly, Los Angeles — 23 | 11

Nº of Novels ⬤ Nº of Short Stories ⬤

Alex Cross - 1993–2021
James Patterson, Washington DC — 30

EUROPE

C. Auguste Dupin - 1841–1844
Edgar Allan Poe, Paris, France
 3

Jules Maigret - 1931–1972
Georges Simenon, Paris, France
75 28

Aurelio Zen - 1988–2007
Michael Dibdin, Rome, Italy
11

Com Salvo Montalbano - 1994–2020
Andrea Camilleri, Sicily, Italy
28 29

Martin Beck - 1965–1975
Maj Sjowall, Per Wahloo, Stockholm, Sweden
10

Kurt Wallander - 1997–2013
Henning Mankell, Ystad, Sweden
12 1

DI Henk Grijpstra & DS Rinus de Gier - 1975–1997
Janwillem van de Wetering, Amsterdam, Netherlands
14

Arkady Renko - 1981–2019
Martin Cruz Smith, Moscow, Russia
9

D.I. John Rebus - 1987–2022
Ian Rankin, Edinburgh, Scotland
25 31

Harry Hole - 1997–2019
Jo Nesbø, Oslo, Norway
12

Detective Erlendur Sveinsson - 1997–2014
Arnaldur Indriðason, Reykjavík, Iceland
14

Thóra Gudmundsdóttir - 2005–2012
Yrsa Sigurdardóttir, Reykjavík, Iceland
6

REST OF WORLD

Ci Chen Cao - 2000–2019
Qiu Xiaolong, Shanghai, China
11

Benny Griessel - 2004–2020
Deon Meyer, Cape Town, South Africa
8

Precious Ramotswe - 1998–2022
Alexander McCall Smith, Gaborone, Botswana
23

Shunsaku Morie - 1990–2013
Taku Ashibe, Osaka, Japan
16 50

DICKENS'S **LONDON**

*More than any other author, Charles Dickens mapped England's capital city
in his novels, and while many districts reappear in different novels, some
are specific to the stories of Oliver Twist, David Copperfield and Pip.*

Where and how many times action
happened in particular postcode

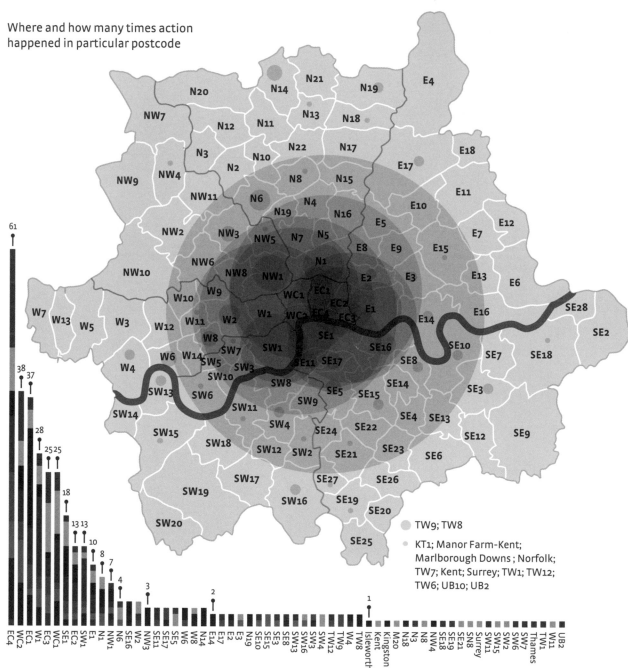

TW9; TW8

KT1; Manor Farm-Kent;
Marlborough Downs ; Norfolk;
TW7; Kent; Surrey; TW1; TW12;
TW6; UB10; UB2

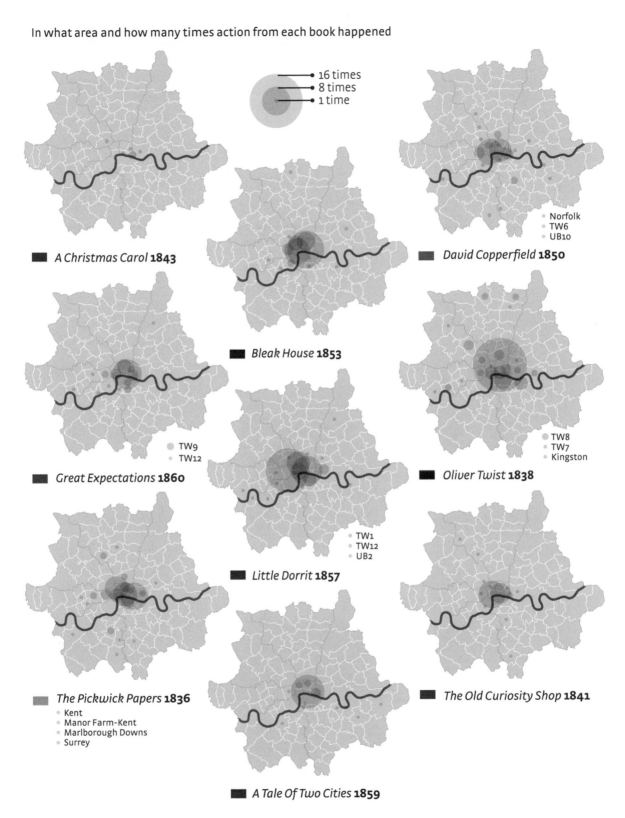

In what area and how many times action from each book happened

16 times
8 times
1 time

A Christmas Carol **1843**

Bleak House **1853**

David Copperfield **1850**
- Norfolk
- TW6
- UB10

Great Expectations **1860**
- TW9
- TW12

Little Dorrit **1857**
- TW1
- TW12
- UB2

Oliver Twist **1838**
- TW8
- TW7
- Kingston

The Pickwick Papers **1836**
- Kent
- Manor Farm-Kent
- Marlborough Downs
- Surrey

A Tale Of Two Cities **1859**

The Old Curiosity Shop **1841**

MINT JULEP

2½ oz bourbon
ice
2 sugar cubes
4–5 mint leaves

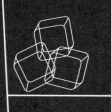

F. SCOTT FITZGERALD
The Great Gatsby
1925

APPLEJACK MARTINI

1 dash grenadine
1 oz lemon or lime juice
2 oz apple
brandy

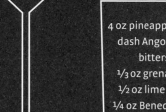

ERNEST HEMINGWAY
The Sun Also Rises
1926

CUBA LIBRE

2 oz white rum
4 oz cola
crushed ice
lime wedge

ERNEST HEMINGWAY
To Have And Have Not
1937

SINGAPORE SLING

4 oz pineapple juice
dash Angostura
bitters
⅓ oz grenadine
½ oz lime juice
¼ oz Benedictine
¼ oz Cointreau
½ oz cherry syrup
11 ½ oz gin

HUNTER S. THOMPSON
*Fear And Loathing
In Las Vegas*
1971

SCOTCH MIST

2-3 oz scotch whisky
or bourbon
½ cup of
crushed ice

RAYMOND CHANDLER
The Big Sleep
1939

GIMLET

½ glass gin
½ glass Roses' lime juice

RAYMOND CHANDLER
The Long Goodbye
1953

WORDY
COCKTAILS

MY PIN

½ glass
pineapple juice
½ glass gin

VLADIMIR NABOKOV
Lolita
1955

DAIQUIRI

¼ oz sugar syrup
¼ oz lime juice
1½ oz light rum

GRAHAM GREENE
Our Man In Havana
1958

CHAMBERY CASSIS

3 oz dry vermouth
½ oz crème de cassis
splash of club soda
crushed ice

ERNEST HEMINGWAY
A Moveable Feast
1964

GREEN ISAACS SPECIAL

1 oz gin
2 oz coconut water
squeeze of lime
dash of bitters

ERNEST HEMINGWAY
Islands In The Sun
1970

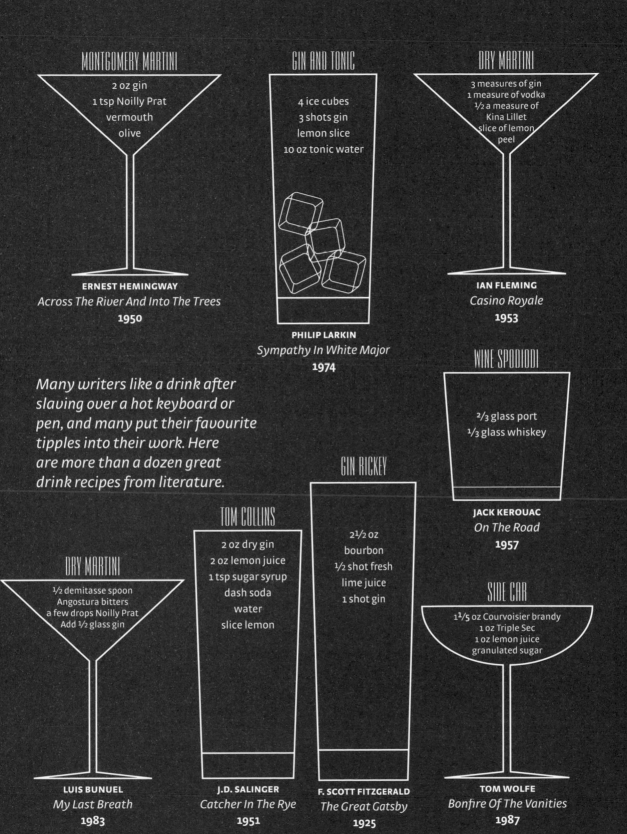

MONTGOMERY MARTINI

2 oz gin
1 tsp Noilly Prat
vermouth
olive

ERNEST HEMINGWAY
Across The River And Into The Trees
1950

GIN AND TONIC

4 ice cubes
3 shots gin
lemon slice
10 oz tonic water

PHILIP LARKIN
Sympathy In White Major
1974

DRY MARTINI

3 measures of gin
1 measure of vodka
½ a measure of
Kina Lillet
slice of lemon
peel

IAN FLEMING
Casino Royale
1953

Many writers like a drink after slaving over a hot keyboard or pen, and many put their favourite tipples into their work. Here are more than a dozen great drink recipes from literature.

WINE SPODIODI

⅔ glass port
⅓ glass whiskey

JACK KEROUAC
On The Road
1957

GIN RICKEY

2½ oz
bourbon
½ shot fresh
lime juice
1 shot gin

DRY MARTINI

½ demitasse spoon
Angostura bitters
a few drops Noilly Prat
Add ½ glass gin

LUIS BUNUEL
My Last Breath
1983

TOM COLLINS

2 oz dry gin
2 oz lemon juice
1 tsp sugar syrup
dash soda
water
slice lemon

J.D. SALINGER
Catcher In The Rye
1951

F. SCOTT FITZGERALD
The Great Gatsby
1925

SIDE CAR

1⅕ oz Courvoisier brandy
1 oz Triple Sec
1 oz lemon juice
granulated sugar

TOM WOLFE
Bonfire Of The Vanities
1987

FREE YOUR MIND

Since ancient times authors, poets and playwrights have been imprisoned by authorities who didn't like what they wrote. Of course, putting a writer in a cell with nothing to distract them can result in great works of literature being incubated. Here are arguably the greatest prison-based works in history, and the reasons for their authors' imprisonment.

/ One day   ✗ One month   ⫻ One year

SEX

Thomas Wyatt (1503–1542)
Whoso List To Hunt (1557)
ADULTERY

Oscar Wilde (1854–1900)
De Profundis (1897)
GROSS INDECENCY

Eldridge Cleaver (1935–1990)
Soul On Ice (1968)
RAPE, ASSAULT WITH INTENT

Thomas Malory (1415–1471)
Le Morte d'Arthur (1451–1461)
ROBBERY, RAPE, TREASON

Marquis de Sade (1740–1814)
The 120 Days Of Sodom (1785)
BLASPHEMY, SODOMY, RAPE

MONEY

John Cleland (1709–1789)
Memoirs Of A Woman Of Pleasure (1748)
DEBT

Henry David Thoreau (1817–1862)
Civil Disobedience (1849)
NON-PAYMENT OF TAXES

O. Henry (1862–1910)
Short Stories (1897–1901)
EMBEZZLEMENT

MURDER

Jack Abbott (1944–2002)
In The Belly Of The Beast (1981)
FORGERY, MURDER

WAR

Arthur Koestler (1905–1983)
Scum Of The Earth (1941)
P.O.W.

Primo Levi (1919–1987)
If This Is A Man (1947)
P.O.W.

Miguel de Cervantes (1547–1616)
Don Quixote part I (1605)
P.O.W.

RELIGION

John Bunyan (1628–1688)
The Pilgrim's Progress (1675)
BREACHES OF THE RELIGION ACT 1592

POLITICS

Aleksandr Solzhenitsyn (1918–2008)
One Day In The Life Of Ivan Denisovich (1962)
ANTI-SOVIET PROPAGANDA

Fyodor Dostoyevsky (1821–1881)
The House Of The Dead (1861)
DISSEMINATING REVOLUTIONARY LITERATURE

Nawal el-Saadawi (1931–)
Memories From The Women's Prison (1983)
POLITICAL SUBVERSION

Mahmoud Dowlatabadi (1940–)
Missing Soluch (1979)
POLITICAL SUBVERSION

Liu Xiaobo (1955–)
The Monologues Of A Doomsday's Survivor (1993)
POLITICAL SUBVERSION

Richard Lovelace (1618–1657)
To Althea, From Prison (1642)
SEDITION

Daniel Defoe (1659–1731)
Hymn To The Pillory (1703)
SEDITIOUS LIBEL

Vaclav Havel (1936–2011)
Letters To Olga (1979–1982)
DISSIDENT

Boethius (480–525)
Consolation Of Philosophy (AD524)
TREASON

Ezra Pound (1885–1972)
The Prison Cantos (1948)
TREASON

Breyten Breytenbach (1939–)
The True Confessions Of An Albino Terrorist (1983)
HIGH TREASON

Voltaire (1694–1778)
Oedipus (1717)
INSULTING THE CROWN

Niccolo Machiavelli (1469–1527)
The Prince (1513)
CONSPIRACY

Antonio Gramsci (1891–1937)
The Prison Notebooks (1928–1934)
CONSPIRACY

THEFT

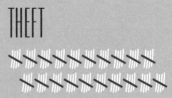

Malcolm Braly (1925–1980)
On The Yard (1967)
THEFT, BURGLARY, ROBBERY

Jean Genet (1910–1986)
Our Lady Of The Flowers (1943)
THEFT

Chester Himes (1909–1980)
To What Red Hell (1931)
ARMED ROBBERY

François Villon (c.1431–c.1463)
The Testament Of 1461
BURGLARY

OTHER

Jack London (1876–1916)
The Road (1907)
VAGRANCY

Credits

Produced by Essential Works Ltd
essentialworks.co.uk

Essential Works

Art Director: Gemma Wilson
Commissioning Editor:
Mal Peachey
Editor: Julia Halford
Researchers: Naomi Barton,
George Edgeller, Phil Hunt,
Jane Mosely, Maria Ines Pinheiro,
Kimberley Simpson, Renske Start,
Jackie Strachan, Giulia Vallone,
Barney White.
Layout: Louise Leffler

Designers/Illustrators

Meegan Barnes (16–17)
Giulia De Amicis (34–35, 132-133)
Barbara Doherty (10–11, 14–15, 18–19, 28–29, 32–33, 38–39, 40–41, 58–59, 60, 66–67, 70–71, 82–83, 84–85, 100–101, 110–111, 130–131)
Jennifer Dossetti (21)
Maya Eilam (44–45)
Cristian Enache (12–13, 50–51, 52–53, 64–65, 68–69, 102–103, 104–105, 120–121, 128–129)
Dan Geoghegan (72–73, 74–75, 98–99)
Marco Giannini (62–63, 88–89, 112–113)
Wojciech Grabalowski (24–25, 80–81, 136–137)
Michael Gray (61, 108, 124–125)
Lorena Guerra (20, 22–23, 122–123, 138–139, 147)

Natasha Hellegouarch (142–143, 152–153)
Diana Coral Hernandez (56–57, 114–115)
Tomasz Kłosinski (46–47, 154–155, 158–159)
Stephen Lillie (26–27, 90–91, 106–107, 116)
Mish Maudsley (86–87)
milkwhale.com (54–55)
Aleksander Savic (140–141, 144–145)
Daniele Severo (36–37, 92–93)
Yael Shinkar (48–49, 126–127, 148–149)
Arnold Skawinski (42–43, 78–79)
Berny Tan (96–97)
Ryan Welch (30–31, 109)
Gemma Wilson (117, 118–119, 134–135, 146, 150–151, 156–157)
Anil Yanik (76–77, 94–95)

Answers to page 90–91

Author	Decade of key work	Nationality
Michel de Montaigne	1580–1590	French
Stendhal	1830-1840	French
Edgar Allan Poe	1840-1850	American
Gustave Flaubert	1850–1860	French
Leo Tolstoy	1865–1875	Russian
Mark Twain	1870–1880	American
August Strindberg	1880–1890	Swedish
Henrik Ibsen	1880–1890	Norwegian
Rudyard Kipling	1894–1904	English
Marcel Proust	1910–1920	French
Ernest Hemingway	1925–1935	American
Gunter Grass	1955–1965	German
VS Naipaul	1960–1970	Trinidadian
Robertson Davies	1970–1980	Canadian
Karl Ove Knausgaard	2000–2010	Norwegian

Answers to page 106–107

Author	Prime period	Nationality
Jane Austen	1800–1815	English
Mary Shelley	1818–1830	English
Elizabeth Barrett Browning	1840–1850	English
George Sand	1830–1860	French
Colette	1900–1945	French
Virginia Woolf	1915–1940	English
Karen Blixen	1926–1956	Danish
Simone de Beauvoir	1940-1970	French
Doris Lessing	1950–1990	English
Maya Angelou	1970–1980	American
Toni Morrison	1980–2000	American
Herta Muller	1980–2000	German/Romanian
Donna Tartt	1992–2013	American
J.K. Rowling	1997–2007	English
E.L. James	2011–2013	English